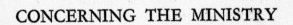

CONCERNING THE MINISTRY

CONCERNING THE MINISTRY

BY

JOHN OMAN, D.D.

HON. FELLOW JESUS COLLEGE
AND FORMER PRINCIPAL WESTMINSTER COLLEGE, CAMBRIDGE

Author of
Grace and Personality, Vision and Authority
The Natural and the Supernatural
etc.

STUDENT CHRISTIAN MOVEMENT PRESS
58 BLOOMSBURY STREET, LONDON, W.C.1

First Published April 1936

Printed in Great Britain

PREFACE

FOR anything so general perhaps no title could be a very enlightening description. One of my former students suggests *Causeries du Samedi*, and were it not so obvious an imitation of Sainte Beuve's *Causeries du Lundi*, and so similar to titles that have already been used in English, *Saturday Talks* might have passed. They were just talks, with freedom to wander into by-paths, and were the last effort of the week, when teacher and taught had had more than enough of serious lecturing, not on Mondays after we had rested at least from this particular kind of labour. As they were further unattended by any shadow of examination, and the speaker could be at his ease and the student, delivered from his note-book, free to listen or not as he was interested, the result may seem occasionally lacking in the solemnity due to so grave a subject. They were given at the beginning as a sort of *hors d'œuvre* to the whole curriculum, but it has been hinted that they are rather the cocktails. Though they never were so exciting, and some of what was necessary for sustaining the attention of the jaded student has been taken out as beneath the dignity of the reader, it may still be necessary to ask that allowance should be made, in the circumstances, for the weakness of human nature, which cannot always be at concert pitch.

The absence of serious systematic treatment was also due to the purpose intended. In a vague way the subject of preaching had been allotted to us, and something more was usually said on it, which, being useful only for the special situation, has been omitted. Though what remains has still to do with preaching, it is in so wide a sense as to make it misleading as a title.

Concerning the Ministry is the best I can do, though it has the opposite defect of being too wide, because the subject is mainly only the human side, especially intercourse with life and men and books—the divine side being the business of all the rest of our course.

5

What concerns the Ministry, and that mainly on its teaching side, may seem only of professional interest. But "like people like priest," and a concern in the people to have the right teachers would do more to provide them than even concern in the teachers themselves. In the Church, as in the State, the greatest of all gains would be the general determination to discover and the general discernment to recognise " men of understanding who know what Israel ought to do."

Except for the merest jottings in a note-book, I had no record of these talks, and, when about to retire, I thought I should like something fuller before it passed from my memory. My secretary tried reporting my last deliverance. Partly the very uneven pace, partly the disturbance of the liberty of prophesying by the sense of being reported, and partly the distractions of bringing my work to a close, made it only a moderate success. So far as this was a source, it was only of the earlier third: and most of this and all the rest had to be fished out of my own recollection with the aid of the notes; and as much of it was *obiter dicta*, without any indication in the notes to aid the recovery, my only memory of it is, like the fisherman's of the fish he hooked but did not catch, as better than anything in the basket.

As, when writing, it was intended only for myself, I was not careful to omit what was personal, and now that I have been persuaded to publish, there is more of this than I care to see in print, however right it may have been in speech. Some has been removed, but it was too much woven with the warp and woof for effective elimination. As I trust I have not greatly transgressed hitherto, mitigation of sentence may be given to a first offender. There is also a good deal of reminiscence, which, though most of it has been changed from that form, may still be too obvious. Yet what is so far back in time seems ancient history and no more personal. As often before, I am indebted to my old friend, G. W. Alexander, for reading the proofs.

JOHN OMAN

CONTENTS

CONCERNING THE MINISTRY

I

THE CHOICE OF WAYS

FROM three sources men's lives are made better or worse. First, there is the influence of their surroundings; second, the effect of their actions; third, the power of their beliefs.

Some ascribe everything to the first: a man is just what his environment makes him. Some ascribe everything to the second: a man, in the end, is just what he does, his environment being what his actions make it, and his beliefs mere vindications of his actions. Some ascribe everything to the third: what is truly believed selects environment, determines action, and moulds character.

All are of vast importance, but if you wish the highest and most profitable service, you must determine which is greatest and, in the end, most effective.

First there is environment.

This may not be all that was claimed for it in the days when it was taken to be the explanation of all evolution, but to realise the enormous effect of its influence you have only to think how much we owe to the organised industry and order and institutions of the society which has clothed us and sheltered us and educated us. Therefore the people who devote their energies to making a better world by better laws, a better economic order and more effective institutions, have much to say for themselves when they regard this as the one concern of supreme importance.

The Church, or, if you will, all churches, for this is the matter on which they are most one, do more to stir interest in this kind of welfare and to produce the people who patiently labour for it than is recognised, and thereby justify their existence as institutions which create a favourable environment. And while the Church, merely as such an institution, would not be the spiritual fellowship which the Apostle took to be the pillar and ground of the truth, this does justify concern for it as an organisation. There is always the danger of taking the institution to be the end. Like its Master, the Church should be as one that serveth, while, as an institution it has often been very much one that sitteth at meat, and, to protect this privileged position, has done things in His name in appalling variance with His spirit. But on the whole, even to-day, there is no other institution with so many prepared to give service and take risks for public righteousness. Wherefore, even if this kind of better world could be called into existence directly by legislation and organisation, it would be worth while being a member of some branch of the Christian Church, though, if you thought it the shortest and most practicable way, you would not care to be a minister in any of them, or even to spend your time working through them, if you could be a leader or even a camp follower in some kind of social movement.

Second as to action.

What men do, and the customs, habits, practices and standards they produce in doing it, are of an effect so great and obvious that many regard action as the supreme, even the sole, concern; and, thinking that action can be controlled directly, devote their energies to amendment of the poor laws and factory acts, and temperance legislation and anti-gambling campaigns, and societies for compelling honesty in business.

The churches are sometimes spoken of as mere obstacles. To hear some people talk one might imagine that to be a professing Christian is to be the most nauseous kind of hypocrite, and that there never was a shady transaction done in the land except by one of them.

Like all else on earth, churches have their failures; and a high profession made incredible by low actions does add reproach to baseness. And though in these days religious profession is not a very fashionable cloak, there is such a thing still as 'a high religion and a low morality.' Yet if judgment were made, not by selecting special, possibly singular instances, but by the whole effect, there is no Christian church which could not face, in this matter of uprightness, any other unselected body of men. Of most Christian congregations it could be said, as an outsider said of my old one, " They have their faults, but, after all, the word of every man among them is as good as his bond; and the women are better than the men." Even the vaguest relation to the Christian congregation does much to maintain industry, to keep families united and homes pure, and people friendly without drink and without gambling.

An official of a criminal court became an earnest worker in his own church because one day it struck him as the most amazing fact that scarcely, in all his long experience, had any member of any church ever been charged with crime, much less had it proved against him.

If you believed that practice in this sense of outward action is the supreme end you might still, therefore, be a member of some Christian church. But if you thought it immediately attainable by outward regulation, you would not wish to be a minister in any, and, above all, would have little interest in preaching, but regard the supreme sphere to be the House of Commons, and the next best Hyde Park.

Yet by their effect upon action a church and a ministry are rightly judged : and it may be that our shortcoming at this time is, largely at least, due to restless ministries, with cheap, sentimental preaching, which has never faced the long demand to make the man of God complete, thoroughly furnished unto every good work.

Finally as to belief.

Belief, in the very commonly accepted sense of what has been imposed on men and they have merely not taken the trouble to reject, may be of some effect, but it is not the faith which removes mountains. When it is still less, and is merely lack of courage openly to repudiate, it is not faith at all ; and the terrible things done in the name of the Church to make this courage difficult, only put a premium on hypocrisy, and denies the freedom with which Christ has set men free.　But if belief is what we accept with our whole heart, and what we are ready in freedom to venture on, does it not determine, above all else, both the world we live in and how we live in it ?

Environment is not merely what we see with our physical vision.　It is still more what we see with the eyes of our soul—our imagination, our insight, our values, our inspiration, our faith in God's mind in it, and His purpose with man in the midst of it.

Nor is practice only what we do.　Thinking is a very important kind of acting, and so is what we love and hate. If action is not the outcome of faith in what is true and good, but is mere obedience to rule even the wisest, or following custom even the best, or respect to good rules even the most exacting, it may be good practice in form but not in substance.

If this be so, is there any shorter cut to a better world than the roundabout way of faith ?

In any case, it is the only way of seeking it in freedom, because all else is imposed from without.　There have been days when 'liberty' only needed to be shouted to be a battle-cry, for it seemed at once above all other possessions and the sole security for any.　To-day it is denounced as mere licence to go astray, and our own faith as the way of seeking it is thought to be hopelessly round-about and to lead to chaos.　Compulsion is regarded as the one strong cement for building an enduring structure of society, and is to be applied at once without any humbug either about faith or freedom.　But time will show again, as it has done so often before, that men cannot long be compelled by anything except what they truly believe, that where there is no vision the people cast off restraint, and that where there is true faith resting on vision, there is no demand they will not obey and no sacrifice they will not make.

The most patent example is political freedom. When I was a student a great crowd of us were addressed by some very distinguished people—Browning and Lowell and Helmholz and Virchow and Pasteur and Lesseps and Saffi. But what I most vividly remember was said by Lavaleye, the Belgian economist. He began, he said, by being of the school of Mill, with everything determined by supply and demand, with freedom mainly in political safeguards for freedom of exchange. But one day he was struck by the singular fact that all Christian countries, with the possible exception of Russia, were in some real sense free, and that no other country was so in any sense. Then he saw that freedom depended, not on political safeguards, but on the people for whom freedom was dearer than life, and that this went back to the great demand, " Let a man deny himself."

But no man can deny himself, even to life itself, which includes all other denials, except by a faith that is greater not only than himself, but than all earthly good. Thereby alone he so rises above himself that, for him, all things are possible, and, even if he is overwhelmed in defeat, he still knows that he will triumph. Has any great victory ever been accomplished on the earth, except by those who had a faith which made them not fear them that kill the body ? Whether they knew of it historically or not, the oriflamme of all the true leaders of man's progress has always been the Cross, the supreme affirmation that not the worst ills of life can deny or defeat the truth, the righteousness, the love of God.

It is not a question of this among other things, but, for the preacher at least, of this above everything. Yet it is only above everything if the faith is high enough and deep enough to do the other things by making action right and the world a better place.

You may not confine this faith to any kind of Christian profession. Everyone lives in a spiritual situation we can call his church, and it means more for any power that is in him than he knows.

The institution of the Church is narrower than this,

and it may be largely by its own fault that it is so much narrower. It has too much appealed to the submissive, not the independent, spirits; it has paid too much attention to comfortable worldliness and too little to the old test of preaching the Gospel to the poor, and making the blind see and the deaf hear; it has too easily accepted tradition and custom, and lacked insight and high courage, both intellectual and spiritual; and it has too highly esteemed those who are strong in respectability and prudence, and not known that Christ came to seek and save the lost and be a physician to the sick. Its fan, too, may be in its hand, but its winnowing of chaff and wheat is not always His. In every form of it as an institution there are many defects : and perhaps no one has any right to be in the ministry who is not conscious of them, even in his own branch of it, and who is not out to remove them. And you should think the Church worth all trouble to amend, as well as to serve, for, if it could commend effectively its own Master with His own freedom, it would overcome most of the dangers that beset both men and nations. For one thing, will any distribution of material goods ever work from without like His kingdom within, with its valuation of things for men, not men for things ? For another, are not the rights of the weak even for the bread that perishes, strong only if we are all children of God in the family of God ? Were it only for economic justice, therefore, it might be a greater gain to capture the Church and see that it is loyal to its own purpose, than to capture and amend even the State.

Yet, for you, the Church should not be any institution. It is the fellowship of faith which is the pillar and ground of the truth.

This influence of faith is what is meant by the kingdom of heaven being as leaven hid in three measures of meal until the whole is leavened. There are congregations which have been just such leaven in the whole community, lifting it to something like their faith, and thereby sweetening and purifying all the life around it.

Seldom, however, have congregations had this distinctive character and influence without the long ministry of some one man behind them. He may have been no great man, but he was a man of great faith in the highest and deepest things of God and the human soul, as he saw them in Jesus Christ. He may not have had a great outward success, but it is the small stream which has power that turns the great mill-wheels which make the nutritious flour, not the wide river, unrippled by motion. The greatest work of faith which ever helped to make a better world was committed to a handful of disciples, not very learned, not supremely able, not very courageous, but men of faith by a vision of God's rule they had seen in their Lord.

II

A PROPHET OF THE PEOPLE

Even able and good men may fail through not taking their business rightly in hand. In the ministry this may be summed up as the wrong way of being like and of being unlike other people.

First we shall consider how you should be like what, at least, other people ought to be.

To begin with, you should be like your most methodical brethren in the ordering of your work.

This is the more necessary that you have no task-master except yourself, who is either the hardest or the easiest, and seldom anything between. If for no other reason, you need order in your work that you may not be under either King Log or King Stork.

First as to King Log. Your work is more irregular than most men's. You cannot work so many hours a day according to a schedule. You have unexpected calls and interruptions. There are many varied tasks which cannot all be done to-day, and you are tempted to put off also to-day's work till to-morrow. Wherefore, all the more you need the discipline of regular methods and habits of work.

More than most men, also, you depend on inspiration. You can do easily and well at one time what you do laboriously and badly at another : and you ought to value by quality, not quantity. The effect of this may be that you become creatures of moods and impulses. Through this alone many come to grief. The gifts, according to the grace given, vary for each of you, and for each of you from time to time. But for this very reason you must wait on your ministry, not by going to sleep and expecting your inspirations to wake you like morning watchmen, but as those who are looking for their Lord, to open to Him at a time that is of His choosing, not yours. Everything may come to him who waits, but it depends on how he waits, whether ploughing his field in winter or only expecting to reap in harvest. The more you depend on inspiration, the more you need to learn to work steadily through the uninspired.

This discipline of regular habits of work is so necessary for all other disciplines that I may be excused if what I say has more insistence than originality. It ought to be a commonplace that the foundation of a good life is good habit, but what is not of such general recognition, especially by those who lack it, is that there may not be bed-rock on which to lay it. The natural provision may be more like the blue putty, called gault in our part of the country, which needs a vast deal of reinforcing. With this, it does not make any worse foundation: and it is part of the task of knowing yourselves to learn how hard a discipline your soul needs. And remember that some of your gifts may themselves be dangers—such as fertility of idea, fluency of expression, ease of speech, great activity. As Plutarch says, " Perhaps the precept, ' know thyself ' would not be considered as divine, if every man could easily reduce it to practice."

An old doctor said about his own calling, that practice is very fine and necessary, but only if you know what you are practising. Otherwise it is mere blinding routine. " I believe, sir, in the midnight oil." The ministry, too, without hard study, can become a deadening routine. But my faith is rather in having your loins girt early with the lamp of day burning. And it may be well to gird your loins physically as well as mentally.

Even in this matter, however, I would not be dogmatic. You have to discover your own best method of working. In managing even yourself, remember that a rough hand is not necessarily a strong one, and that it

B

is not weak for having a delicate, sensitive, persuasive touch. To know yourselves, even in small matters, is extremely useful knowledge. Do your work, by all means, as you can do it best. Yet do not be persuaded that your best work is in deshabille in the small hours, merely by the seeming ease with which you put it through your hands, for it may only be that your critical faculty has gone to sleep.

Even now, as students, the midnight oil is mostly self-deception. You write easily because you are not alive to its defects, and you read easily because you swallow uncritically what is before you. But it will become more so when you enter upon your ministry. A busy doctor may have no time sacred except late, but even the busiest minister will find that people will respect his morning hours if he is known to be in his study as other men are in their offices and workshops. They will not, however, respect any other hour of the day. A few ingenious people will discover that your study in the morning is the certain place and time for finding you. Yet they seldom persist in interrupting you about nothing of consequence if they find you obviously at your work : and if it is of consequence, you must, of course, endure it at any time. Then, if you have visited in the afternoon and had a meeting or two in the evening, you cannot be in your first freshness, or perhaps able to gird your loins for any kind of serious work. And if you put it off, not to next morning but to next night, the time will come to be the Greek kalends.

Wherefore, it may be well to imitate your lay brethren who have to go to their work at a fixed hour in the morning, and pay some exact heed to that common article of household furniture—the clock. Anything very heroic, such as five o'clock summer-time, might give too exalted a sense of superiority to common habits to be good for your soul. But a favourite figure of Jeremiah for God's earnestness about the salvation of His people is rising up early to speak to them. This he uses no less than nine times, and as six of them are to send His prophets, naturally His prophets should follow His example, at all events to the extent of not being behind the shopkeeper or bank clerk. Let us say, breakfast at eight, and in your study, girt physically and mentally, by nine. In short, you must be like your industrious brethren by starting the day as though you meant to do a day's work, not only with time before you, but with concentration for the employment of it.

Though you should not be too sensitive to physical conditions, and one man's meat may be another man's poison, we all have our helpful circumstances. Buffon is said to have arrayed himself in court dress before he sat down to write : while Grub Street, though it could only visit its friends on clean-shirt days, had the freedom of Olympus and could wield the thunders of Jove even on the days when the solitary garment was at the washing. Yet the average man has very much the same experience of meats and poisons, and you would probably not be aided by a court dress, even if you possessed such an article ; and probably clean linen has so much become a habit, that you would be disturbingly self-conscious without it. Wherefore, it may be best to imitate once more your lay brethren, in being presentable without being conspicuously adorned. Few, at least, work as well in slippers as in shoes, and when you feel particularly slack, some virtue may pass into you by putting on your boots. Anyhow, a man who wanders into his study in the middle of the morning, unshaven and in dressing-gown and bedroom slippers, is in about as perilous a state as one who takes to secret drinking.

To sum up, you should be like your most efficient lay brethren in learning well your own particular job and being a master in it.

Only faith, hope and love are abiding, and for this task in particular, the greatest of these is love. Without it even faith is nothing, and prophetic gift and understanding of mysteries, and all knowledge, less than nothing.

Even now knowledge is passing away, if only into fuller knowledge. Wherefore, you have to realise that there may be humble and even ignorant people who have found, better than you, the more excellent way. The Lord may still take the authentic prophet, like Amos, not from any prophetic school, but from the herdmen and fruit-gatherers, and you may not say to him " Prophesy not "; and it is a grave defect in the Church not to have more hope of his coming and a more recognised place for him.

Yet the schools of the prophets transmitted and taught the teaching of Amos, and made the work of all the prophets continuous. Even the more excellent way is not to hinder you from coveting earnestly the best gifts ; and the only effective way of coveting is to work for them. That genius is the faculty of taking pains is a very inadequate definition, but even genius accomplishes very little without it, and with this faculty you can go a long way towards making up for the lack of genius. Moreover, you are to think of all that is true and honourable and just and pure and lovely, virtuous in itself, and worthy of praise ; and though hard and continuous work is at present rather a heresy, these things are not to be thought through, much less done, without it.

Though you should have no professional feeling in the matter, and though any protection for any profession, save the merit of its equipment, is of doubtful benefit to the public and of certain harm to itself, you cannot justify the position of being set aside to give your whole time to the ministry except by being equipped for it in a way impossible for those to whom it is only an occasional exercise. And this is mainly to be done by cultivating these lesser, but essential, gifts.

An old Scottish professor used to say that there were three qualifications for the ministry—the grace of God, knowledge of the Scriptures in the sacred tongues, and gumption. The first, he said, we have the promise of if we pray for it, the second we can have if we work for it, but if the last is not a gift of nature he did not know that either prayer or labour could provide it. Your gifts are your calling, and wisdom is the first qualification. Yet, as the Apostle prayed that his readers should grow in wisdom and practical discernment, even though he regarded the word of wisdom as a divine gift and different from knowledge, he was evidently not quite so pessimistic about advancing in it by prayer and work. Knowledge of God's word in all its manifestations, in life and history and the world about us, is more than the most exact knowledge of Scripture, even in the sacred tongues. Though it is a good foundation, in this, as all else, the greatest is love, and as love and work should be one, you would do well to take for your motto Victor Hugo's last words, when, at the point of dying, he thought he was addressing the children—" Aimez et travaillez."

Moreover, in these days, no church does much in the way of discerning diversities of gifts, but all ministers are expected to be apostles and prophets and teachers and workers of miracles and healers and speakers and interpreters and as this necessity is laid upon you, you may covet, with the earnestness which does its best, to attain them all.

Our business is not with those who are born preachers. Should you be thus endowed, you need not confer with flesh and blood, though, considering the danger of approbation, possibly of adulation, to which this may expose you, a short time in Arabia might be well spent. We do not profess to produce the man who mounts up with wings as eagles. On the contrary, we have to take great care not to clip his pinions. All we can hope to do much for is the man who can walk for a long day and not faint.

Yet, looking down the long vista of many years, I see him not only lasting longer, but going farther. So many who start with a flourish, after a short flight come down, though mostly they escape on the parachute of betaking themselves elsewhere.

Some things you can be taught, but the most important you must teach yourselves, and to indicate what these might be will occupy most of our time.

But King Stork needs to be faced as well as King Log : and, though you may not know it at present, he may prove to be the tougher customer of the two. Few men, I think, fail in the ministry by not spending enough hours on it. They see the light that it is good, but they have not, like God, divided the light from the darkness, and so their lives are a sort of twilight, not of the gods, but of fussing, with much cry and little wool, from one drab and dragging drudgery to another. Concentration is far more important than time, and you cannot stick into your work unless you know when to stop it. " All work and no play makes Jack a dull boy " : and many ministers have become very dull boys indeed by having no place for play or even rest. Even natural human laziness cannot be crushed too ruthlessly without loss.

Your bow should always be ready for bending, but it will lose its elasticity if it is always bent. Continued power of interest and application is largely the power to change the interests and slacken the tension.

In reading Gladstone's *Life* nothing impressed me so much as his power of hard work, except his command of the secret of it, which was his power of throwing off the burden of it when he was done. For example, when the national expenditure went over a figure which would seem the height of parsimony in our extravagant days, he wrought for weeks ten hours a day to moderate its swelling port, and then had to see the Queen in what proved to be a stormy interview. Yet he walked out of Balmoral and went over the Perthshire hills with the gay inconsequence of a boy in his teens.

Unfortunately you cannot always shut the shop at six, nor can you observe one day in seven on the proper day. But you ought to put up the shutters some time every day, and you should keep one day in seven, preferably the second day in the week, as it cannot be the first. Possibly there is more truth in what someone has said than some of us who have not observed the rule too well would like to admit, that ministers are often such poor creatures because they do not observe one day of rest in seven. If so, they belong to a very large company at present, but, as has also been said, a general error is merely a general plague to which many succumb. As life goes on you will find this task of working when you work and playing when you play increasingly difficult. But you will also find it increasingly necessary, for one of the first duties of advancing years is to stand up against the tyranny of dull drudgery. And precisely when the calls are most urgent, you need most relief if you are to meet them effectively. It was at the moment of His greatest seeming success, when so many were coming and going that there was no leisure so much as to eat, that Jesus said to His disciples, " Come ye apart into a desert place and rest a while."

In the second place, you should be like your most genial brethren in the freedom and wide humanity of your intercourse.

This follows the last point more closely than you might suppose, because, unless you have done your own work strenuously and have finished with it, you will never have leisure for other people. Scott's astonishing power of getting every kind of person to talk to him was largely that the work he had begun at five was finished at one, and then he was free to spend his time almost entirely in human intercourse. Only a mind which does its work with concentration and then can leave it, has leisure to come truly into contact with other people. Easy intercourse is impossible if your work is spread out in thin diffusion over all the day.

Few differences are greater in men than this touch with humanity or the absence of it. One person can come into any atmosphere and it at once becomes genial ; another can pass through a young people's Christmas party like a block of ice. Before you complain of the chilliness of the atmosphere, remember that the neighbourhood of an iceberg is always cold.

A mind at leisure from itself to sympathise is the first condition. But it also requires the liveliest interest in man just as man, and care not to allow stereotyped judgment, even moral judgment, to replace insight. When this happens you would not have a ghost of a chance of discovering that the publicans and harlots may go into the kingdom of heaven before the respectable, and except you know and love the common people, they are not likely to hear you gladly. Nor may you ignore those who seem definitely hostile. There are still Jews who reject Christianity because it does not travel their road, and Greeks who reject it because it does not suit their superior minds, but you have to be a Jew to the Jew and a Greek to the Greek. This meant for the Apostle, at least, that he knew how to establish human intercourse with them. To begin with, he sought them where they were to be found, the Jew in the synagogue, and the Greeks in the school and the market-place. Yet, if it came to the Sanhedrin and Areopagus, he was ready to face the music. To-day I suppose that would be Oxford and the Royal Exchange. The Greek who spends his time only in telling and hearing some new thing, in the former place, is apparently still remarkably open for religious discussion, but the Jew by nature, in the latter institution, the Apostle himself would find difficult to approach.

Probably you will not be called to enter either sphere, but the Greek, as one who finds Christianity foolishness, and the Jew, who finds it a stumbling-block, are always with you, if you live in the wide world of men and do not confine yourself to ecclesiastically minded persons of your own type of piety. Even among this sheltered band they may exist, but they would be so masquerading that you would not recognise them. Moreover, the bravest, no more than the basest, flourishes in religious green-houses.

Further, the Apostle not only went where the people were, but he took them as he found them. Becoming a Jew to the Jew and a Greek to the Greek did not mean the much admired diplomacy of saying what each would like, such as preaching against circumcision to the Greeks and against idolatry to the Jews : but it did mean that he began with what they could understand, and such imperfect religion as either happened to possess, and led them on by such persuasion as, from their own standpoint, they might think convincing. He started with unknown gods and heathen poetry with the Greeks, and with the Law and the Old Testament with the Jews, and neither reversed the process nor used one stereotyped approach.

No one more than the parson ought to have an easy approach to all his fellow-mortals ; but perhaps to no other calling is it more difficult. Sometimes it is ascribed wholly to clerical attire : and this can be used to ward off the shock of people speaking profanely or irreligiously, to the end of living in a fool's paradise, or rather a young ladies' boarding school. But of all people, one who would minister to their spiritual needs should know what people are when their speech utters their thoughts. Unfortunately an official religious relation is much easier to cultivate than a human. But the main hindrance is not the dog-collar on the neck, but what has been called the dog-collary mind, which would only shout parson at you the more loudly for being dressed in a kilt and a pink tie. Anyone who takes his calling seriously seldom escapes the marks of it, and, within due limits, there is no reason why he should. But there is a great difference in the kind of professional parson he is taken to be, whether one who, as Seeley described him, regards God as the head of the clerical profession, or one who in all his ways plainly shows that he regards God as the Father of all men. Though you may never become adepts at meeting all kinds of people each on his own ground, like the Apostle, if you have the same idea of the God and Father of all, and the same interest in men as made in His image and your brethren, you will not ignominiously fail.

To-day you can have the aid of many treatises in pastoral psychology. The people that has written more on psychology than all other peoples together does not seem to have received much aid from it in understanding

actual people in actual situations. Seeing by general
rules and theories is using spectacles which blur the
individual and characteristic.

You had better go to the Great Teacher and learn by
example. My old pupil, Dr Manson, thinks he has discovered three quite distinct modes of address—one
suited to the common people, one to the disciples, and
one to the scribes and other learned persons. Whether
this be true or not, it is certain that Jesus knew not only
what was in man, but in the man before him. He
saw the worst in him with a depth and clearness beyond
the reach of any psychology of the morbid, but He
also stirred to life and action qualities of insight, devotion,
and goodness, far beyond what any psychology perceives
as normal. And not merely the normal of what he is,
but the supernormal he may become, is the true man.

> If not above himself he can
> Exalt himself, how mean a thing is man.

And to his real greatness he can neither exalt himself
by himself nor for himself.

Perhaps, too, you will be told that you should know
economics as well as psychology. No doubt the Master
had a good deal of practical knowledge of it, though less
of the stewards of great men owing thousands than
poor housewives sweeping the house for a copper.
Yet nothing is more manifest in all His actual dealings
with men than His utter indifference to their economic
status. And for you, too, there is only one essential
mastery of economics you need, which is to have the
aristocracy of mind which treats the duke and the ditcher
alike, both as the duke, though, as with Jesus, slightly
more in favour of the ditcher.

There is a new catchword which calls you to be
Life-changers. But you had better begin by being
Life-understanders, for it is mere impertinence to set
out to change what, for all you know, may be better
than what you propose to substitute for it. Nor, when
you do know, may you have merely your own, perhaps

rather mechanical, way of setting about the transformation, for even God proceeds by 'manifold wisdom.' Moreover, as no one should be according to standard, even the life you may legitimately wish to change should not be refashioned according to your pattern, but to the full realisation of its own particular reflection of the infinitely varied image of God.

Finally you should be like your most religious brethren in the ordinary Christian life.

First, its daily practice.

From many temptations no doubt your calling will protect you. You are not likely to be tempted by drink or gambling or shady transactions : and you may easily underrate what has to be resisted by other men and forget that your security may not be superior virtue, but merely absence of temptation, not love of God and your fellows as inspired by Jesus Christ, but fear of man as inspired by Mrs Grundy. Yet the ministry has its own temptations, and if we take our Lord's estimate of sins, as the more deadly for being of the heart and not of gross outward manifestation, they may be the greatest man has to undergo. Apart from vanity and slackness, there is the danger of professional religion, which is perilously akin to hypocrisy, of the voluntary humility which is conscious of merit, of taking ordinary loyalties and risks to be self-sacrifice, of losing your freedom and ease and joy and enterprise, of putting yourselves on a pedestal as an example, and, above all, by having no message to your hard-pressed, burdened, struggling fellow-men, because you have not yourselves won the victory of peace.

Second, the simple things of faith.

You cannot, perhaps, take the things of faith as simply as other people. You ought to know the difficulties better than they do, and you have to take in much of your knowledge in more critical and abstract ways. Yet in the end you must discover that nothing is so difficult to achieve as simplicity, and that the source of it is sincerity in living as well as thinking. You best approve things that are excellent by living excellently in them. You have not to prove but to manifest the existence of God. Questions even about the Gospels are a small concern compared with knowing, by living in it, the world in which Jesus spoke. It is not theories of the Atonement that matter, but knowing that the more we are sensitive to sin, the more in Christ we find peace.

Third, its regular nourishment.

Fixed habits are useful in this as in all other matters. They may become a tyranny of regulations or a mill-tread round of routine, which you should not allow even to the best habits, but if you have not the good habit of methodical application, you will be apt to fall into the bad habit of no application at all. Exercises like family worship and your own praying with your Father in secret, for example, are apt to pass into disuse if they cease to be of regular observance.

A minister cannot help reading his Bible, and if he can read it in the original so much the better. Yet you may with profit follow what is said to have been Conington's practice of reading the English Bible for purposes of edification, just because it enabled him to lay aside the scholar and become the simple Christian.

With respect to other devotional literature I speak with hesitation : because, while I have read with profit such classics as Augustine's *Confessions*, and *The Imitation*, and *Grace Abounding*, and even some much more emotional and mystical literature, they constantly seem to miss the human, gracious, calm, objective enterprising religion of Jesus Christ. But should you come to any such conclusion, let it be only by your own judgment, and only after first benefiting from studying them with care. Nor would I ask you to accept my estimate that I find a more natural and spontaneous venture of faith in Luther's *Freedom of a Christian Man*, John Woolman's *Journal*, and the *Life of Mary Slessor*, except to the extent of giving them a trial. Yet the parched spirit may more readily go to the poets than to any of them for the water of life.

Most important of all is that Sunday for you should be a day of edification and refreshing as much as for any of your congregation, because you worship with your congregation, and do not merely conduct services for them, and preach to your own souls as much at least as to other people's.

III

A PROPHET TO THE PEOPLE

THAT yours should be a prophetic ministry may seem too high a claim for any ordinary man, who knew himself, to make. Yet it is not larger than the actual requirement. Even in the humblest exercise of it, you have to account of yourselves, and account highly.

Among human vocations, however, it should not be singular for this reason, because nothing great was ever done without accounting of oneself in undertaking it. Yet, while it is of oneself, it is not from oneself. Goethe speaks of a 'demonic element' in men of genius, some sense of possession by a might greater than their own, something of destiny, something of Napoleon's conviction that the world still turned for him. Though in a very different temper, faith is just such a trust that the world still turns for us. When it asks, " Who is sufficient for these things ? " it is not concerned about their height or difficulty, but only as to whether they are in God's service in answer to His call. Then it can say for all that comes that God makes all things work together for good to His ends and our achievement. This alone is true confidence in accepting any call.

The essential question, therefore, is the call. In this also the ministry should not be singular. I know a medical professor who says that a man has no more right to be a doctor without a call than to be a minister. Law may not seem so obvious as medicine. But I have a school-fellow who is a lawyer, of whom his wife said, not in complaint but in pride, " You can't expect him to find it a very fat job, when his one idea is to prevent people from going to law, by settling their quarrels with friendliness and commonsense." A profession, thus called

to see that 'the fruit of righteousness is peace,' would
be as noble in itself and as profitable for society as any
ministry of teaching or healing. Every vocation, even
the humblest—which is often the most useful—should
be according to the gifts and calling of God, for only
when a man has the work for which these fit him, can
he either have joy or effectiveness. The Aberdonian
gardener who thought that it took a man from his county
to be a real master in the learned professions, such as
ministering, doctoring and gardening, no doubt was of
excessive local patriotism, but he had an admirable and
proper pride in his job, which might be extended to
every other with great gain to the community. One
of the saddest changes of our time is the increasing
extent to which men are made mere cogs in the machine,
and can have no pride in their own individual creation.
Yet things need not be as bad as they are, if jobs were
not chosen for their immediate profit, but by the gifts
and the calling of God they exercise.

You may not, therefore, distinguish your own vocation
as sacred from all others as secular. Every calling has a
sacred side if men lift up their hearts to it, and your own
also has a secular through which you, like others, should
manifest the sacred.

That the gifts and calling of God are without repentance means, I suppose, that they will not let you down
if they are trusted. The gifts themselves may be the
call; and the call is for the exercise of the gifts.

But what modest man, you may ask, can assume that
he has the gifts to show that God has sent him among
some who are prophets? Should you have such gifts,
you are accountable for them, and, therefore, must
account of them. Yet nothing is further from vanity,
for what have you that you have not received? A man
may no more be vain of his intellectual or moral gifts
than of his possessions. The former are given in trust
to be used, as much as the latter, and you may not undervalue them in face of life's challenge and opportunity,
any more than you may undervalue your material

possessions in face of the tax-collector. With the
Apostle, you must say, " By the grace of God I am what
I am," and realise how this sets you free from false
modesty as from false pride.

No one is without

> That one talent, which is death to hide,

and no one should have to say of the smallest that it is

> Lodged with me useless.

The one talent is often used more vainly, as well as more
feebly, than the ten. Yet it may also be so used as to
go further than the ten timidly, slackly, irresponsibly
employed.

With any gifts, however, there must be the call. You
may not have had any vision in the Temple, or have
heard any voice saying, "Whom shall we send and who
will go for us?" or any voice in your heart compelling you
to reply, " Here am I, send me," in face of what you may
know, as Isaiah did, to be large failure and small visible
success. It may be much more like Jeremiah's, "O
Lord God! I cannot speak, for I am a child." Probably
any call you have is rather what you cannot escape,
than what you enter upon with high assurance. Yet,
none the less for that, God may put His word in your
mouth, " to pluck up and to break down, to build and
to plant."

Perhaps you are rather troubled at this stage as to
your vagueness concerning what a ministry ought to be.
Ought you not to have at least some clear ideal of it?

I was once asked to give a paper at a conference on
" Our Ideal of Life." When I agreed, I did not imagine
that the task of defining life's ideal would be easy, but
I thought it ought to be attempted. What the paper
came to in the end, however, was that I had discovered
that I had no ideal of life ; and what was more, that
it was not my business to provide one. Most of my
audience thought this a most humiliating confession for

a minister, a dabbler in edifying literature, a teacher of theological students. My answer was that I had been a great swell at setting up ideals of life up to fifteen—my chief ambitions being to sail a boat in a gale and ride a horse bare-backed—but that life, increasingly ever since, had proved too uncertain a proposition. I did not want to be a minister, but somehow could not escape. If I had had an ideal of the work, it would have had no resemblance to the job I was set to. I never wrote a book by conscious purpose but one, and it was bad, even for me. The others just came somehow and insisted on being written. As a teacher I have never got beyond doing my best for each person as occasion offers.

You should not say with Luther that God led you like a blind horse, for, though you may never have seen far enough to plan, there was always the fairly clear distinction of the higher and the lower way, and if you took the higher, there was never any doubt, however it might appear for a time, that it was the right decision, because it was following a wiser ideal for life than one's own. The higher however your aspiration, the deeper your thoughts, the more, it may be, will the plan of wise love in your life be a riddle only dimly guessed. Shallowness and self-satisfaction may deliver you from all problems and all perplexities, though God's guidance is too much on the steep upward path to give you any such deliverance. Yet in the assurance that God's love knows you however imperfectly you know it, you find just the upward path makes joy and strength as well as perplexity and labour.

This faith you will find simple people in your congregations applying to life, with a wisdom and a courage from which you will have much to learn, and as they too are the Lord's prophets, you may not find any essential difference from them.

Yet, while there is no true prophet who lacks ordinary humanity, there is also no true prophet who falls into the ordinary views and ways of acting. In this sense he can only help the people as he differs from them.

c

" For the Lord spake thus to me with a strong hand, and instructed me that I should not walk in the ways of this people, saying, ' Say ye not, A conspiracy, concerning all whereof this people shall say, A conspiracy ; neither fear their fear nor be in dread thereof.' The Lord of hosts, him shall ye sanctify : and let him be your fear, let him be your dread." This was the experience of the ancient prophet : and it should not be different with the modern. " He that believeth shall not make haste." " In quietness and confidence shall be your strength." This means, neither be worried nor flurried, neither dread evil nor engage in endless schemes to defeat it. What could we do more for our restless age than give men some taste of this, even one day in seven ? And how shall we give what we do not possess ? Wherefore there are few things so much required of us as that our souls should behave and quiet themselves within us as a weaned child, and just allow life to speak to us till we hear the voice of God as the central calm within all hurry and change.

What it means is best seen in our Lord's own ministry. His life is often set forth as if He started with an ideal of His work and then planned His life and death. But is not the heart of the whole manifestation of the Father that He took life just as it came ? His sense of vocation was to accept men and events as God sent them, and find the Father's whole purpose in them. The incidents He met were often trivial, but consider how He used them. Most of the people He met were such as we meet every day, but consider what He saw in them and brought out of them. Even the crucifixion met Him as what He could not avoid if He was to go on with the work given Him to do.

Schweitzer gives a picture of a short ministry of Jesus as one succession of excited expectations and enthusiastic endeavours. Sit down and read through the Gospel of Mark, upon which he mainly relies, and you will find not only a man of peace, but a man of leisure. He never preached the gospel of peace in a flurry. All His teaching speaks of leisure, not only from itself and from the world, but even from His ministry.

To teach in parables at all meant leisure. He noticed the flowers and the sky, and the farmer at work, and the children at play. Then think of what leisure He had for people when they wanted to see Him. They found Him disengaged and at ease and ready to have a quiet talk with them. He did not hurry to prescribe for them and then say, " Now you must go, I have a long list to get through to-day." He said, " This is how I look at it. Now, what do you think about it yourself ? " Then He often left them to themselves and their own thoughts, yet only after He had taken time and trouble to show them what their real thoughts were.

It is worth our while to ask what was the secret of this busy but leisured life.

Though there is also another reason, what concerns us here is what He calls His yoke.

The yoke is sometimes expounded as if it were itself a burden, a sort of harness in which we are dumb, driven cattle. But a yoke is a piece of wood, hollowed to fit the shoulders, so that a weight can be carried with the whole strength of the upright body, and not with the mere strength of the bent arms. The measure of the relief is the extent to which it fits easily. Only because His yoke is easy, in this sense does Jesus mean that His burden is light. He never thought that life could be blessed by diminishing its burden of high responsibility and great endeavour. The real fruitfulness and nobility of life depend on the greatness of the burden we can bear, which is nothing less than all that God requires of us. What makes it light is the way we bear it : and this is the easy yoke, under which we can stand up, ungalled and straight and strong.

This is to be, like Him, meek and lowly in heart. Yet it has nothing to do with the 'gentle Jesus, meek and mild' of the sentimental hymns. How anyone who ever read a Gospel should come to this idea of the mightiest, most resolute, most courageous leader in the battle for the highest is hard to say. His is the meekness which inherits the earth because it accepts utterly God's will and finds the true uses of the earth in God's purpose, and so is mighty to do as well as to endure. So far is it from being submissiveness to man, that God so fills the whole horizon as to leave no room for any other judgment. It is the joy of the Lord, the assurance, unhesitating, unquestioning, that His requirements are alone wise and good, which is the strength that makes the heaviest burden light.

Courage of any kind makes life a less distressing and more successful battle. Even physical courage is not to be despised. Fear is the most paralysing of all emotions, and 'cowards die many deaths in fearing one.' If, like Knox, you can look in the face of angry men and trying situations, and not be 'overly afeard,' many dangers which beset the timid will never rise for you.

Long ago, when I was at the beginning of my way, one who had been many years at the work told me that handling a congregation is like handling dogs, they never bite you till they see you're frightened. And handling most things is like that. Dangers and trials often come merely because you are afraid of them. If, nevertheless, they do come, they will be about something worth fighting for, and the brave man is strong against them simply because he never dreams of running away, and the coward is defeated from the first because his first idea is to escape : and the moment he shows the smallest sign of running away he is lost.

In the end, however, it all comes back to moral courage. A young lad who had been very badly wounded in the war said, " There is an appalling lot of bunkum talked about courage. Anybody can do anything in a crowd, and especially if he entirely lacks imagination to realise danger till it hits him in the face. There was a man in our company who never could hear a shell pass without ducking and shivering, but if it came to going on alone he was the last man of us who would turn back." This victory of the spirit over the flesh is alone true courage. It is not the absence of fear, but victory over it.

The supreme victory is not to fear them that kill the body, and no liberty—political, social, intellectual, religious—can be won or maintained at smaller cost. Yet this is made possible only by the faith that liberty is dearer than life, and this can only be faith in spiritual good above material. Wherefore, we should speak of faith, not courage : even though it is not faith unless it is also courage, for we only truly believe what we immediately and necessarily act on.

It is this immediacy and necessity which is the power of our Lord's promise. To be meek and lowly in spirit is to know that the earth is the Lord's and the fulness thereof, and that therefore there is no sure guidance in it except His will and no road impassable through which it leads. But most of us see this only dimly, and act on it only after reflecting on all it involves and on what people will think. This is the lump in the yoke that makes it gall, the reason why so many are weary and heavy laden.

But when doing right is one with knowing it, the amount and variety of work done, mostly for others, is amazing, though not so amazing as the cheerful and even gay heart with which it is done. The more thus undertaken, the more the burden seems to become lighter. Thus, and not by evading any of the necessary duties of your calling, should you have a right to preach peace because you are yourselves men of peace. Without it you will be little help to any burdened spirit. Even for your business men, the last thing that would help would be to become yourselves business men, with your mind bent on running your church as a going concern, all the more if you regard it as simply your own concern and assume towards it unlimited liability.

IV

ENEMIES OF LEISURE

Nothing really good or abiding can be achieved without quietness and even leisure of mind, and of no work is this truer than your own.

Possibly you may be looking forward to the ministry as the sphere, above all others, where high thinking will not be encroached upon by lower interests, and high emprise for the eternal not be crowded out by small pre-occupations with the temporal. But the day may come when the idea of leisure amid life's ceaseless claims may seem the suggestion of an ignoramus, and quietness of spirit amid its distractions a hopeless ideal.

In the far-off days when I was a student a German fellow-student told me that a German pastor was "Allermenschen Mädchen," meaning 'Everybody's slavey.'

Luther told Christians to be the servant of all men, but as he also said that they were to be the freest of all men, probably that was not his idea of service. Yet, even in this, we trust, free country, it may be your lot, unless you take very energetic means to escape.

You may find yourself regarded as conveniently at home, with any amount of time and energy at your disposal, while other men are away all day, credited at least with being busy. Moreover, is it not your business to be friendly and sociable, to be interested in all schemes for human welfare, and to give your support to all kinds of religious organisations? You do your best not to disappoint good people, and presently you find yourself esteemed as an ornament at tea-parties, a valued member of local committees, an indispensable speaker at religious meetings. Then in your congregation you have a few admirers who think you the Admirable Crichton at doing everything just as it ought to be done. Have you not such a head for business? And, unfortunately, in spite of the business man's settled conviction that this capacity is confined to his own class and that ministers have less than the least ordinary modicum, ministers are often quite gifted in that way. Should this be your case you find all kinds of details slipping into your hands. You are dragged into congregational finance; you find yourself organising secretary rather than minister of the congregation; your reputation is noised abroad, and you are found to be a useful person for the donkey-work of church committees, till you have, not, like the Apostle, the care of the churches, but—a very different matter—their cares, mostly material.

In your present happy possession of the cheerful confidence of youth, and perhaps greater ignorance of Satan's devices than St Paul's long and varied experience had taught him, you see an easy way of escape from such a fate. Cannot you say ' No ' ?

But ' No ' has always been an extremely difficult word to a genial person; and in these days of telephones it is not becoming easier. You have no time to hunt up an excuse before replying, for the hesitation of a moment suggests that you are trying to invent one. The necessity of consulting your engagement book only gives a few minutes for reflexion, and leaves no escape, because you know you have committed yourself unless something actually stands on the exact date.

Yet when it comes to the ancient device of the personal interview, you may even feel grateful for the modern. Sometimes your caller is one who obliges others so constantly that you cannot find it in your heart to do anything but oblige him if at all in your power. Yet he is not the worst, for if you say you can't, out of the generosity of his heart he will at once believe you, and, being himself a busy man, he will not interrupt you more than he can help. A much more troublesome person is of the type which has been described as having the higher Christianity, which knows that it is more blessed to give than to receive, and wishes you to have the benefit. He comes when he knows that you are busiest, because then he can talk you into submission in order to get rid of him. To agree is as foolish as the woman who married a man to be shot of his importunity, but I know, by sad experience, the weakness of human nature.

Yet if your sole concern is to see the work done, and not in the least the figure you cut in it, there is a better way than having everything in your own hands. One reason why people who have done most efficient work in all walks of life are quiet and even leisured, is that they know how to choose, to inspire, to make responsible their helpers. Your particular work should be just calling each one to his own ministry, and the more you succeed, the better for them, for the work, and for yourself in waiting on your own central ministry.

Wherefore I am going to give you what may seem shocking advice. Never do yourself what you can persuade other people to do, even if you think it only half as well done. Take the other half as allowance for your little vanities ; and never appear in anything unless necessary ; and never take credit if it can at all reasonably be passed on to other people.

Much distracting work, however, has to be done, and you may not evade any of life's real calls to service. It will be no praise to your ministry to have an ill-organised congregation, to limit your interest to its members, to miss any opportunity for helping anyone, to take no interest in your own church and the Church at large, or even the world at large.

Nor is the busiest life hostile to the best work, if you know how to take it.

Goethe says that genius breeds itself in solitude, character in life's troubled sea. Though broadly true, neither verdict is to be accepted without qualification.

On the one hand, great thoughts and high inspirations are no doubt born in solitude.

The Muse nae poet ever fand her
Till by himsel' he learned to wander
Adown a trottin' burn's meander,
And no think lang.

But, also, no strong, independent, true character ever comes to birth except in solitary wrestling with serious thought and noble aspiration and high resolve.

On the other hand, genius finds its sphere in the busy haunts of men, not in the wilderness. Its message is to men living in the world, and its inspiration from the world to which is speaks.

The Public Orator once said that it is a first principle of Cambridge criticism that nothing was ever put into a book for the first time. And German criticism occupies itself still more with literature in terms of written sources. Yet nothing is of high interest except what appears for the first time : and that is from life, not books. Moreover, little of the world's greatest literature has been produced by merely literary men. The author of Job was certainly no recluse. Could Dante have written the *Divina Commedia* had he not been a great patriot ? Shakespeare wrote his greatest plays amid a busy life as an actor and theatre-manager, and in keen response to the stirring events of his time. The deepest poetic interest of *Paradise Lost* comes from the struggle for a rule of God on earth through which Milton had passed as an active participant ; and *Samson* is a song of spiritual victory after the visible battle seemed to be lost. Goethe himself, though perhaps the most detached of poets, took an active part in public business and social affairs, and was certainly no recluse. Victor Hugo did much of his best work in exile, whither patriotic zeal had driven him.

But your work as a preacher has more to do with character than with genius ; and character, though it is also born in solitude, comes to strength by buffeting life's troubled sea. That " in the long run," as Whitehead expresses it, " your character and your conduct depend upon your intimate convictions," that " your character is developed according to your faith," ought to be the firm conviction of every preacher. Therefore his business is with faith, and that is "what the individual does with his own solitariness." Yet it is all barren and unreal, unless it issue in the character which is more than conqueror in face of life's demands, either of endurance or enterprise : and you will help no one to victory if you yourself shun the battle.

This may go so hard with you that you may lose all hope of any harvest of a quiet eye and of any solitude for it to bless : yet the hindrance is much less work than the wrong way of doing it, which may be summed up as flurry and worry. Flurry dissipates energy, worry loads it.

I begin with flurry and its well-spring, which is self-importance.

The supreme device of Satan is to confuse busyness with business and to make self-importance wear the aspect of humble service. You are flattered by these calls upon you, you enjoy sunning yourself in the public estimation, you plume yourself on your reputation when you see your name in the local and religious press, you feel yourself a really public person when you are on committees for organising other people. With your eye turned to the figure you cut in your work, you will forget that doing many things is not doing much, any more than saying many things is saying much.

This is by no means confined to the ministry. In many walks of life there are people who waste life in trying to persuade themselves and other people that the earth would not turn on its axis unless they scurried from one thing to another on its surface like an ant that has had its hole stopped. Yet the ministry offers exceptional opportunities and temptations.

The chief temptation is that this is the view of your work most easily and widely appreciated by others, even though it be not your real, central work at all, but mere distraction from it. To the outward observer your real work may appear mere idleness, even if it were mortal conflict with all the powers of darkness. And if you do not forget the figure you cut in your work, by being absorbed in the one purpose of doing it well up to the utmost measure of your ability and as judged by your own conscience in the sight of God, you will not be able to close your eyes to this external estimate of your labours. You will spend more time arranging your books than in reading them, and in referring to your engagements than in keeping them, and you will develop a trot that does not cover half as much ground as an easy swing, and a babble of words that does not say half as much as one quiet phrase.

Then the ministry becomes a succession of ' one blamed thing after another,' and whatever happens to be nearest your eye at the moment will fill the horizon, though it may be utterly unimportant.

' Hurrying to and fro ' is not to be commended in any case. Yet there is something to be said for ' seeking some great thing to do or secret thing to know.' What has no commendation is hurrying to and fro after what is not worth doing or knowing.

Though no one of you, I trust, is likely to achieve this full blight of fussy self-importance, there is always danger in the mildest beginnings. Once you esteem yourselves phenomenally busy men there is the possibility some day of taking the fluttering of the washing on the clothes-line of self-importance for eagle's wings soaring in the empyrean.

Though quietness and leisure need times of freedom from being always busy, it is flurry which is the worst assault upon them. With a quiet mind and a leisured spirit you may have calm at the centre of any storm ; but with flurry every claim loses its proportion and every activity becomes a storm in a teacup.

The other device of Satan is worry, which can appear as an angel of light to the sensitive soul and the tender conscience.

You are not so ignorant of what lies before you as not to know that there are few ministries to-day in which you can find deliverance by having nothing to cause anxiety. Even in the old days people spoke of the black-coated proletariat: and ministerial stipends do not go as far to-day as then. To keep a struggling congregation above water was never easy; and it was perhaps never so difficult as now. Physical toughness and buoyant spirits are great assets for meeting trouble: but the day may come when your health is uncertain and your heart is sad. There are difficult people and difficult situations. While you are young you may distrust your experience and prudence in dealing with them; and when you grow older you have less strength to bear with them and no greater assurance of wisdom in dealing with them. The time may also arrive when you find yourself less fresh, less spontaneous, less fruitful in ideas, less energetic in presenting what you have. Then there may fall on you grave responsibilities, often of the most intimate nature, which you must bear alone: and you may be of the people to whom the possibility of mistake can become a nightmare.

Each one knows where his own shoe pinches, and no one else does. Therefore, it is easy to exaggerate the difficulties of your own calling compared with others; and one of the first qualifications for the ministry is to be sensitive to other people's troubles and anxieties, which you cannot be if you are worrying about your own. Yet it may not be easy to escape, because there are few ministries to-day which may not be the most appalling worry, if once a man let himself go.

But worry is not work. It is merely friction. Proverbs are mostly very wise sayings, and few are truer than that it is worry, not work, that kills. The servant of the Lord should not worry, any more than he should strive, not even over responsibility. There is a vast difference between a sensitive conscience and a neuralgic one. A sensitive one is concerned only with knowing what is right; a neuralgic, mainly with anxiety about whether we are right. This is the worry above all others from which you will need deliverance.

It is true that you may not evade responsibility even

by casting it upon the Lord. You must also bear it as your own burden. The Apostle does not pray that God would make people's decisions for them, but that He would give them spiritual wisdom, which means discernment of the principles of life and conduct, and spiritual understanding, which means power of applying them to practical situations. Life would be no gymnasium for the sons of God if He gave men their decisions by mere flashes of inward illumination. You have to give the matter your most careful, well-informed, unbiased consideration, then leave it with God, knowing that, as nothing more is in your power, nothing more is in your care. And this is as true of what you ought to speak as of what you ought to do. Speaking, remember, is a very important kind of action : and preaching which is not action is mere fustian.

Worry is not mere shortcoming. It is a denial of your ministry. Unless your faith in God is consolation and peace and victory in your heart within and your situation without, what have you to offer ? Here you test your working, everyday religion as perhaps nowhere else ; and here, too, you most prove your value for your hard-pressed, burdened, struggling fellows.

Yet you may sometimes learn far more from them in their shining cheerfulness in all kinds of narrow circumstances, illness, and old age, loneliness and distress, than you will ever be able to teach, because they point you to the great example, the Master Himself, who took life as it came and as no one else ever did made the most of it, and showed that the very worst it could bring was still of God.

If you see in the Cross the victory over evil which enables you in everything to give thanks, you will no more be impressed by your meritorious activities or talk of self-sacrifice. "Don't send us," James Chalmers the missionary said, " fellows who talk of self-sacrifice. Send us those who take danger and difficulties as the pepper and salt of life."

Moreover, all this is very relevant to your preaching. What makes Christianity attractive in the ordinary church-goer is just humanity, cheerful patience, a humility which neither asserts itself nor defers too much to human judgment, kindness, consideration, self-forgetfulness, sympathy, understanding. And the spring of no man's ministry ever fails or runs dry in which these shine.

V

A MINISTRY OF RECONCILIATION

ONE secret of our Lord's quietness and leisure, was the unquestioning acceptance of God's mind, undistressed by wavering and indecision. This we learn by coming to Him, though not merely for precept nor even for example. We are to come because He manifests the rule of the Father, through word and life, as of utter kindness even to the unthankful and evil, of unrestricted forgiveness and of quite unlimited mercy, of a knowledge which numbers the hairs of our head, of a wisdom which sees the end from the beginning, of a goodness which refuses no good gift to His children. Therefore, we cannot but be meek and lowly in it because it is a rule of love, wherein there is a peace the world cannot give or take away and a purity which sees God even in this evil, suffering world, above all, in all, working through all. Thus to commend God's love to us, in face of all that could be against us, occupied all His life as well as transfigured His death, so that, in it all, God was in Him reconciling the world to Himself.

The other secret of His peace was in what He did not do as well as in what He did. What delivered Him from life's fitful fever was that nothing else concerned Him except the friendship with God which makes all burdens light. If He could not make men friends with God He did not seem to think it worth while doing anything less. He would not have troubled to cross the street to make the most disreputable publican into the most respectable, church-going Pharisee. He never started any anti-anything campaign. His attempt at reformation in the Temple was unique, and seems to have been, what we should all be the stronger for having occasionally, just an outburst of natural indignation at seeing merchandise made of religion. But He otherwise kept to His own rule. "Resist not evil," which does not mean 'Don't fight,' but 'Don't waste your strength and devotion by skirmishing with evil in detail.' Evil is weak by its own nature and only flourishes by the absence of good. Therefore labour for the good and let it replace evil !

If I did not know it before, the war taught me how right He is. No kind of merely accepted religion was worth anything : whereas any real religion and true sincerity, even much perplexed in faith and faulty in practice, came through amazingly.

But how much on which we spend our energies is just resisting evil ! How much is just trying to reform publicans into Pharisees ! In this whole matter we have received, not our Lord's religious and moral judgment, but the external judgment of the world. How much that all our churches are trying to do did not interest Him at all ! How much that interested Him is expected by us to be a mere by-product of our other activities !

St Paul conceives his own ministry as the carrying on of this work of his Master, by what he calls both Christ's good news and his own, because it is his own assurance of God's quite unconditioned love through Christ who died for us while we were yet sinners, not as the sole condition of God's forgiveness, but to commend God's love toward us as quite unlimited in its forgiveness and mercy. Thus equipped, we are ambassadors on behalf of Christ, as though God were entreating by us, "Be ye reconciled to God."

Reconciliation sounds a large theological term, but it means simply coming to ourselves and arising and going to our Father. As the essential significance of reconciliation is that it is to God " of whom are all things," restoration to friendship with Him makes all things new. It is peace, not by feeble submission and cowardly surrender, but by the assurance of supreme generalship now and of victory in the end, which gives strength and valour. It is not a sentimental relation to a remote spirit in the heavens, but a practical dealing with all things here and now, with the basest in human nature as no denial that any man is made in God's image, and with the ghastliest events as no denial, in spite of all that man has done with it, that the earth is the Lord's. For ourselves it is, in particular, reconciliation to our discipline and our duty, and being enabled in everything to give thanks, which is the only real fulfilment of the First Commandment to have no other gods before God. Had not ' all things ' included so much that is dark and terrible nothing so ghastly as the Cross would have been needed to commend God's love to us through ' all things.' As it faces every ignominy and every wickedness nothing needs to be excluded.

In the sense that this manifests a relation to God by which all things work for our highest good and all things are ours, it is a finished work, though not in any way of finality. Its quality is to enable us to go on even when we only see in the rusty mirror of our own lives the broken reflection of our Lord's, and only guess as in a riddle that love rules amid our own imperfect walking by it, in the assurance that, though we do not know this rule of love, it knows us. The very essence of its eternal purpose is that it is what eye has not seen, nor ear heard, nor has it entered into the heart to conceive. Even another life is not for the Apostle a finality, but only the blessedness of knowing this rule as it now knows us.

This combination of what, because it is uncertain in outcome must be definite and decided in attitude, we have in the three incidents recorded in Luke ix. 57-62. Jesus is not there saying, " I have a distressful life, and have broken with human ties, therefore you must." This would be inhuman and hard. What He is saying is that even following Him is not a fixed order, but a road on which we must ever leave the past behind and face forward, yet where the only failure to reach God's end is turning back. Had the saying, " The Son of Man

D

hath not where to lay his head," referred to Jesus in particular, He would have contrasted Himself with the happier lot of other men, not with birds and foxes. As elsewhere, it means man in general. 'He looks before and after and sighs for what is not,' because 'God has set eternity in his heart.' Wherefore earth cannot provide him any nest or lair in which he can rest content ; and Jesus warns this man that even following Him is no such finality. Though man is but the creature of a day, 'all that God has done from the beginning to the end' concerns him. Thus while he walks on a little spot of earth, the vastness of the sky, which makes even earth unending, is over him, and this is his greatness, even as it is his ceaseless endeavour and his unresting challenge. Just for this very reason the summons is to the future, and with decisiveness we are committed to its trials and its tasks : and just because there is no finality in the outcome of life, the sole guidance is the rule of God. Preaching the kingdom is just preaching the unknown as God's gracious purpose, and the known as His immediate guidance.

Seeking finality in religion is trying to walk on the sky, and expecting it in earthly things is denying that the sky exists.

The glory of God's rule is that it is for an end beyond all our conceiving. But though we do not know the goal, we know that the road is to follow God's guidance day by day. In it we are to walk with the freedom wherewith Christ has set us free, physically, intellectually and morally. This we do by the faith which works by love, the love which is the essential of God's rule revealed in Him. Thereby, and not by any human regulation we are to become one in truth by seeing eye to eye in sincerity, and one in fellowship and service, because we stand shoulder to shoulder in love.

This alone would rescue your souls from much fret and your lives from much fuss : though, if you regard your ministry of reconciliation as only one among other ministries, it will give you only partial deliverance. Yet it has a right to be the sole ministry only if, in the end, it fulfils all the others, in making better people and a better world.

About this the words of a friend of mine should have weight, because, as a working man, he learned the lesson in the hard school of experience. " First and last," he said, " I have been in everything I thought might help the working man. But I now know that you can't have a better world till you have better people ; and that you can't have better people till they are right with God as well as man." If you were really convinced that this is not merely edifying but true, fussy activities would at once fall away from you, and you would have a peace the world cannot take away. Perhaps no one has any right to be in the ministry at all unless he is quite convinced, not only of the value of this way, but that there is no other. Perhaps no one is quite a Christian who is not.

The question is whether there is any other way.

The present production of ideals for our State is even more in excess of demand than wheat, and they are not as nourishing. Some are mere sentimental evasions of the stern facts of life and human nature. When these cannot be evaded the easy way out is to fall back on authority, both in religion and politics. But is this anything save fainting and growing weary in the long journey towards man's true goal of freedom ?

To those of us who spent our youth in the high hope that freedom, conceived as our own glad acceptance of God's rule as our own, interpreted God's ways and was man's highest challenge, it is a sad experience to find that the failure to believe it, which we used to think was the timidity of age, has become the boast of youth. Yet the renunciation is not confined to youth, even now. There are people, and there have always been people, of all ages, who, not really believing that God alone knows the end from the beginning and that we must be free to be loyal day by day and in all relations to what we can discern of His will, cherish the idea of a rigid human scheme, and a strong man or a strong institution to force it upon humanity. Nor have even the leaders of the churches always been able to distinguish between this hasty spirit of the age and the Spirit who rules all the ages.

It is only a step from this to the short-cut which does not go round by the way of God at all, but which preaches that you ought to know what you want and go for it straight, and which holds religion to be a mere fetter on the will and a blight on life. And as for a better world, the very idea of freedom and loyalty and service is a mere drag on the wheels of progress.

Perhaps it will be good for us in the end to be brought thus sharply to the dividing of the ways, for we are far too ready to accept Christianity without asking if it is true and what it maintains as the central truth.

I am not arguing for a capitalistic society against a socialistic or even a communistic. A society in which, though God has given abundance, and gifts to men whereby this abundance can be secured with less labour, we are, like Tantalus, up to the chin in water and cannot drink, and man is enslaved to his job because he dare not lose it, for many can and would work but cannot, is not free or stable.

Were men's chief interests higher and nobler than the bread which perishes, the day might come when we could make common stock of all material requirements, as we do now of air and water. One who has lived much among men who have given their deepest thought and most strenuous endeavour to the search for truth and the production of what they thought might benefit humanity without much concern about its material reward, cannot think gain even the strongest motive; and the effect on those who have made it their main object in life does not seem to prove it the highest. But if man is only an animal, material gain is the highest motive he can cherish as well as the strongest. And he would be lost without it. Moreover, if he is only to be a comfortable and well provisioned animal, why should the strong be troubled about justice to others, and not fight for his own hand and be as rich as he can ?   Only if the weak is made, like yourself, in God's image, your brother seated at your Father's table, does justice for him become insistent even in material things.

Without a higher conception of good, communism would only be another cul-de-sac.   Man seems to progress by trying all kinds of blind alleys : and, if these are farther on, they should be tried.   Whether it is farther on will depend on the spirit in which it is tried. If it is in the present materialistic spirit, it will be a very blind alley indeed, an attempt to make man, like the birds and the foxes, content with their holes and their nests.   If, however, there is any meaning in history, it is that God suffers us to try blind alleys, but not to find finality in them.   God has made man a wayfarer, and he is not likely to be long content to remain where he is by any comfort of his dug-out, nor even by the fear of finding only wet trenches in No-man's Land.   The great and high task of an ambassador for Christ is to reconcile man just to these ways of endless reaching forward because the goal is beyond all time and space.

This is doubtless a great responsibility, requiring much varied resource and the most steadfast application, yet, as it is one task and not many, and the main resource for it is not in yourselves, it is made light by its own peace and by a joy given to concentration on one purpose, which is never possessed by dissipation of energy in multitudinous activities.

VI

THE MEANS AND THE END

THE one means which the Apostle Paul said he ever used was manifesting the truth. But to manifest is much more than merely to announce.

If your work is a ministry of reconciliation, preaching may seem to you, as it has to many, to be a simple business of repeating with fervour and insistence the same message. Have you not just to go on saying, " Now, then, we are ambassadors for Christ, as though God did beseech you by us; we pray you in Christ's stead, that ye be reconciled to God " ?

In support of this view Paul himself is quoted. Did he not say, " For I determined not to know anything among you save Jesus Christ, and him crucified " ? By relating this saying to the fact that he came direct to Corinth from Athens, it has been supposed to mean that he was disappointed with the result at Athens, and in Corinth decided to keep to the simple Gospel and not indulge in any more fine orations, in which he quoted heathen poetry and spoke in philosophic vein of God and man, starting from such indication of religious need as he could discover.

Why should we suppose that he was disappointed or that he could have expected any success at all in any other way ? It is true that he did not see his way to stay longer in Athens. But Dionysius the Areopagite and Damaris, and others with them, would scarcely have meant failure as the result of a single speech to one who had often had no result from many but increase of opposition. How in any other way could he have reached anyone in that audience ? And is he not justifying the method when he says that he becomes

54

to those who are without law as without law? Moreover, in the very Epistle in which he says he is determined to know only Jesus Christ and Him crucified, if
the idea of a plain, direct offer of the Gospel was his
meaning, he evidently kept very badly to his purpose.
There are not more than half a dozen short passages
which could be so interpreted. It deals with parties
in the Church, the true wisdom and greatness, church
discipline, mixed marriages, intercourse with heathen
neighbours, abuses at the Lord's Supper, and there is
the great ode on love, and the psalm on victory over
death. Moreover, in another Epistle he says, "Whatsoever things are true, whatsoever things are lovely,
whatsoever things are of good report, think on these
things."

We are also to do them, but he plainly regarded deep
thinking as necessary for high acting; and if this was
the purpose of his preaching, he obviously did not
interpret 'Take no thought about what you shall say'
as meaning, 'Don't think about it,' nor, of course, could
he, for the Greek means 'Be not anxious,' which, even
for clear thinking, is a very necessary condition.

Augustine is much nearer right when he says that if
Paul knew Christ and Him crucified fully, he knew all
things, though, as Paul never claimed to have all knowledge, it would be nearer the truth to say that he had a
relation to God of whom are all things whereby he could
maintain a right attitude of mind and a right practical
bearing towards all things and all men, in the faith that
we may possess all things as of God for the service of
His rule, and love all men as possible joint-heirs with us
of it. The Cross meant for him the all-inclusive love of
God. What he is saying is that he wishes to deal with
all the troublesome, perplexing, personally distressing
questions, in this sphere and by this power, without
weakness and without animus and as one with a great
sense of debt and not of merit.

The one business of an ambassador is to serve his
country. But if he represent it worthily in all common

speech and action, and manifest its honour in his own honourable life and conduct, he does not need to seize on every person and every opportunity to preach monotonously on its glories in order to be known as wholly devoted to its interests. And when he does speak for his country on fitting occasions, he has to know its true interest and also the interests of the persons among whom he would promote it. The Apostle thinks of himself as just such an ambassador. Though he would have had no sympathy with the definition of his duties in the double sense of lying abroad for the benefit of one's country, but repudiated vehemently the charge that, being crafty, he caught men with guile, and trusted, as few ambassadors do, to utter truth and simple sincerity, he knew that he must be awake to opportunity and dexterous in making the most of it. He does not imagine that he can manifest truth merely by repeating the same phrases without applying it to men's varied lives and make it come home to their vastly different thoughts. In short, he does his best to follow the manifold wisdom of God, with its endlessly varied ways of dealing with men whom He has made in His own image, never by mere repetition of one pattern, but in endless individuality.

Preaching is not the only, not even the highest and most convincing way of manifesting the truth. The people who exercise the greatest religious influence may not preach in public or talk much about religion even in private, yet they are 'living epistles of Christ, known and read of all men.' There is truth in the doctrine of *Yoga*, that you cannot teach anyone religion, but if you live your own religion beside him he may catch the flame. Only if preaching is such a manifestation will life be lit from it. If not, men will say with Emerson, "I cannot hear what you say, what you are speaks so loud." Or as the Apostle expresses it, You may have the tongue of men and of angels, yet be sounding brass or a clanging cymbal.

Large and varied as his activities were, the Apostle

regarded preaching as the special manifestation of the truth to which he was specially called, and he set no limits to its possibilities. Wherefore you also may magnify your office.

But uttering commonplaces, sanctimoniously or even piously, rhetorically or even eloquently, is obscuring the truth, not manifesting it. Speaking about religion by mere reiteration even of essentials does not manifest it. The truth is manifested as it is shown to be the endless wonder of God's living varied world. God's message may be one, but its depth is infinite and its extension all-embracing. And if you feel yourselves straitened, believe that you are not limited in God's truth, but only in yourselves.

This does not mean that you may not deal with the humblest interests of the humblest lives, or that you should always have high-soaring thoughts and never descend to sanctified common sense. You are speaking for the God of whom are all things, and there is nothing in life His friendship does not cover. Therefore, not only is nothing human alien to you, but all of it may shine with the glory of God. The very business of manifestation is to place God's friendship in the midst of all life's thoughts and activities. Nor is nature around us or any created thing to be excluded.

This task is twofold, and your preaching may approach it from either end. Either you can show how great principles of God's wise love have the most practical applications ; or from some matter of life and conduct you can travel to great principles. By both ways you should show that friendship with God comes down into every joy and sorrow, and that every trial and every task are taken up into its strength and peace.

The truth concerns the God and Father of our Lord Jesus Christ and His relation to us and to the world, and our relation to Him and to His kingdom or rule. It is Christ's good news. Yet, as you can manifest only what you have, it must also be your own, made yours by your own mind's insight and your own heart's loyalty, if your preaching is not to be in word only but in demonstration of the Spirit and in power.

In some sense this requires a theology. By this I do not mean a body of abstract doctrine you have learned, but a view of things human and divine which is a central and essential part of yourself. It need not be any finished system, as if you had to have everything cut and dried before starting. Better than cramming finalities down people's throats is to make them feel that they are seekers with you after truth that reaches out to the Infinite. But unless you have an ever more gracious vision of the Father in the face of Jesus Christ, an ever deepening sense of the patient, wise and loving dealing with every human soul, and a growing assurance that, in spite of all that man has done with it, the earth is the Lord's and the fulness thereof, and that His rule is the one enduring reality in it, which informs all your preaching, no eloquence, no cleverness, no learning, even no fertility of idea and illustration will long save it from wearing out.

If, however, your vision is always growing and you are helping people to see it with you, you will find that what other congregations may think only heavy, your own congregations will feel to be weighty, because they are realising in it not the ephemeral but the eternal, and the vicissitudes even of the hardest and perhaps least obviously prosperous ministry may only show more clearly that the truth you manifest speaks of ' the things which cannot be shaken.' Such ministries have been, whose praise was certainly not of men, but it might well be your highest hope that, when you have finished your course, you have as good ground to trust that there would be the praise of God.

Yet manifesting the truth is only a means to an end, which the Apostle describes as commending himself to every man's conscience. As all means should be determined by the purpose it is to serve, so should the way in which truth is to be manifested.

The aim is to commend yourselves, but it is to con-

science and neither to desire nor to dread. Conscience
to the Apostle means what in man, made in the image
of God, responds to truth as well as to right, and you
commend yourself to it, not only by including both
but by combining both in one. Truth does not appeal
to the heart until it is the faith upon which you cannot
but act, and you do not act rightly except upon truth
which is at once convincing and challenging.

That conscience, thus understood, is the one thing
in man to which it is worth while to appeal, is very far
at present from being accepted doctrine. Ruling by
terror, by the might of mass violence, by organised compulsion, by appeal to race and nationality and class,
seems to have received new sanctions in these days.
Working patiently through every man's conscience of
truth and right is so far from being thought the only
effective way of arriving at a better state, and the
freedom which goes with it is so little deemed the one
essential of whatsoever better state may be, that it is
denounced as a hopelessly roundabout way of arriving
nowhere, and appeal to it only a feeble device of the
weak, a mere attempt to throw dust in the eyes of the
vanguard of the strong. Yet this is not new but rather
a reversion to the primitive instincts.

Nor is it absent from religion. Obscurantism is not
the greatest objection to fundamentalist subjection to
the letter of the Scripture, nor fear of revolution to the
demand for absolute submission to an infallible Church.
But the deep offence against the Christian spirit is the
absence of faith in the power of conscience of truth and
right to maintain itself, and trust only in the lash of
unquestioned authority backed by the terrors of hell.
In short, it is not a commending to conscience but an
appeal to fear. Count it all joy that you have very
little of this left you, and that you have no other means
of commending yourselves than the early Christians had
when they went forth to convert a hostile and indifferent pagan world, with no external authority either of
Church or Scripture, or any appeal save to every man's

conscience. Do not forget that the world never saw so great a transformation, and that the Church has never repeated that victory just because it mixed up two appeals which cannot with profit be combined.

Yet you must not confine yourself to anything less than every man's conscience. If you have only your own kind of thinking as students—formal, abstract and doctrinaire—and are not practically concerned with the bearing of the fulness of God's truth on the whole range of human experience, and you have only the sheltered and accepted and respectable ideals in which you have been brought up, hedged round, it may be, by the traditions of your sect and the interests of your class, unaccommodated man may have a right to say that his conscience is not very deeply concerned. You must be sure that your appeal is both divine and human and not mere accepted dogma, and that your ideal of righteousness does not confuse the advantages of education, of good influences, of good form, or of regard for social approval and terror of social consequences, with personal decision and openness to truth and goodness purely because they are true and good.

Nothing is more wonderful in Jesus than the sureness with which He keeps clear the distinction between intellectual and even spiritual privilege and sincere personal response to truth however contrary to accepted opinion, and loyalty which discerns and follows the right however much it be in the shade of human disapproval. This alone has sureness and confidence of appeal to every man's conscience, whatever his condition, theologically or morally or socially.

Set yourselves before Him and ask yourselves whether you really have victory over life when you do not cheerfully take the rough with the smooth ; and whether you are judging righteous judgment when you do not distinguish moral stumbling from spiritual obliquity. A charge frequently heard against the Church is that it approves a person who is respectable from habit and profit and coldness of blood, though he be hard as nails, while it disapproves of a workman who goes 'on the bust' occasionally, though he would pawn his shirt to feed a starving brother or his children. And you may well have the unhappy feeling that it is a right judgment. Are we not a little mixed up about the publican and the Pharisee and what is essential in God's view who judges the heart; and is not the conscience to which appeal is made rather formal and moralistic than at once wholly human and utterly concerned with what God says to it as it stands between two rules, one of which only it can serve?

It has been said that men's faiths are merely fossils of their actions. And men do invent dogmas, above all religious dogmas, to justify their actions. But real faiths, faiths grounded on conscience of truth and right, have immeasurably affected, not only individual action, but the whole organisation of life, so much so that almost all that is now cold, hard, fixed opinion and accepted institution were all at one time made in the furnace of ardent belief.

The prophets made a new world for Israel by their faith in the one righteous and gracious God; Jesus made what the Apostle calls a new creation by His conception of the rule of the Father, and by what He did to help men in face of every ill to believe in it; the Catholic Church made a new order out of chaos by its faith in a God of order working His wise will in the earth; the Reformation made a new world, even for poetry and science, by its faith that the common life is the sphere of God's highest service; Puritanism created a new idea of political freedom by its faith in the rights and the duties of the spiritual man. Nor is this confined to what is normally recognised as religious. The French Revolution had its origin and its power in faith in the rights of man before the Deity. What is really strong in the Soviet to-day is not its ruthless organisation but its faith in a loyalty which, however it denies religion, is religious in quality, and what is weak in it is its failure to raise this to be God's sanction and not merely man's.

The German revolution is still hunting for such a faith, and its greatest weakness is that it has not yet been able to pass beyond theological subtleties.

History, therefore, as well as the Gospels, teaches that faith can remove mountains : and the only question is that its truth should be such that it will be the right mountains it sets itself to remove.

For this there is only one right faith, faith in what God actually purposes with His children in His world and by means of His world, and what in consequence is the measure and the end and the true guidance of life. Unless what we believe is the truth, no matter how consoling it may be, it is vain illusion. In Jesus Christ the Apostle thought he had made sure discovery that it was actual good news of God that He has a purpose with man far beyond man's own knowing, which even life's worst ills can serve, for which gain might be loss and loss gain, and towards which no road, if it be of God's appointing and requiring, can be too hard : and this is either true or it is not true.

Jesus was no ascetic. He was full of the joy of life and He cherished all that was beautiful in Nature and human nature, but He held that even these goods could only be truly possessed as means to yet higher possession : and the joyous sense of all discipline and duty being God's wise guidance towards it was the yoke with which He lightly carried every burden which His life's task laid upon Him even to the Cross. If this is not an actual account of our world and of ourselves within it, then it is mere folly to take the high and perilous road, and all that is left is to get as much as one can, and have as good a time as one can, and shirk as much trouble as one can. But it is evident that you cannot manifest it by mere argument or exposition. The real world we prove only as we live in it, reaching out to its possibilities with all our insight and endeavour.

Faith is precisely that by which we cannot help but live, yet the faith is as essential as the life. The view that nothing much depends on what men think, but only on what they do, forgets that the value of what they do depends on what they think. The worthiest actions are not noble if the thinking is only of fear or vanity.

Jesus is the way to the Father because He is both the life and the truth. How much would His life have meant without His teaching or His teaching without His life? His life shines through His truth even as His truth is manifested through His life, and it is this perfect union which lifts duty from drudgery into inspiration.

VII

PERSONAL WEIGHT

You may think that with this high road before you, lower paths will have no attraction for you. But the quotation, *Video meliora proboque, deteriora sequor*, is so hackneyed because it is so commonly .exemplified. And the better it is, the more our weakness may follow the worse, for it is precisely on the highest, steepest paths that faintness overtakes the traveller. This above all else is the cause of the slow progress of humanity, and, most of all, on the strenuous upward way of attaining freedom in conscience of God's truth and righteousness. From it men have turned in all ages and are now turning into any shelter of authority which promises to be an inn of tranquillity. Fortunately for man, as it is God's end for him, he is never allowed long to rest in it, but by discord and disaster driven out again to the exposed upland. Yet the time may come when, as your eyes grow dim and the mists gather and your heart faints and the world around despairs of the height of God's purpose, you too may feel that it is the mockery of the unattainable and come to think that nearer ends are all that can reasonably be expected of human nature in your circumstances. Then in all your work, but especially in your preaching, perhaps unconsciously, you accept them. As the lower aims are temptations which thus beset you, it may be well to consider what they may be, and all the more that they can appear as angels of light and not, in their true character, as messengers of Satan to buffet you.

The first is to put in the time decently.

You would of course scorn such an idea. But there are such things as going on too long without a spell, being in bad form, suffering from much distraction and many demands, when day after day returns with ' the petty round of irritating concerns and duties.' And then it may be no small achievement to be able to do your day's darg in an honest and workmanlike manner, and on the Sunday morning to be able to utter Stevenson's prayer, " Give us to go blithely on our business all this day. Bring us to our resting beds weary and content and undishonoured, and grant us in the end the gift of sleep."

But with at most two short half-hours at your disposal, amid a long week for your hearers of common interests and worldly cares and abounding temptations, and in face of the vastness of God's truth and the height of His purpose in Jesus Christ, you may not rest content even with your best workmanship, but should live pursuing an aim forever beyond attainment. Here above all is the danger of fainting and growing weary, for there can be no progress in preaching, any more than in any other high endeavour, with a goal you can overtake and with it rest content.

The second is to put in the time pleasantly.

Still more the suggestion that this might be a temptation for you in the least degree may seem to insult your present seriousness of purpose. The trouble is that it is so near what is right and much to be desired.

It naturally belongs to youth to wish to please people, and not even what may distress can be of any value, unless you would have done all you could to please that is consistent with sincerity. It is high praise of Saul and Jonathan that they "were lovely and pleasant in their lives." If for no other reason than that you can do no good till you win a hearing, it is well to be charming persons of pleasant speech, as far as the burden of the Lord allows. You need not think that you are impressive only when you are scowling, and conscientious only when you are scolding. Geniality is a great sweetener of life in the pulpit as elsewhere, and even if you have to

E

challenge and rebuke, it will not go far if it be merely the natural growling of a bear.

Nevertheless, what makes the false prophet in our time as of old is responding to the demand, "Prophesy not unto us right things, speak unto us smooth things, prophesy deceits." When preaching becomes subtleties, prettinesses, touches of pathos, and knows nothing about a Word of God that divides soul and spirit and discerns the thoughts and intents of the heart, it becomes merely an extra cushion in an easy-chair. A great deal of the criticism of preaching and even of the whole church services is that they are not sufficiently comfortably upholstered for elderly people, and not dressed out in sufficiently gay colours to attract young people. But when it comes to this, and there is no overwhelming message of God, no good news that may also shatter false faiths and hopes, it would be better to own up at once that there are more lively places than the church can ever hope to be.

The third is to put in the time vaingloriously.

The suggestion that you should ever be in danger of making this your aim you may think uncalled for and verging on insult. And as a conscious purpose expressed thus crudely, you are not likely ever to set it before you. But in few things is the heart more subtly deceitful than vanity. Cæsar is not the only person who ever lived of whom it could be said, " Then is he flattered most when most I say he loves not flattery." If you become a really popular preacher, able to sway large audiences, it may be a devastating temptation, for the possession of power is so easy to regard as the possession of merit. But while the discovery that you are no brilliant and shining light may deliver you from the worst danger of taking yourselves to be little idols, you have to be as popular as you can, and even a little flattery is a very heady kind of incense if you allow it to be a kind of desire you sniff up like the wild ass. Nor do you need to make a sensation to have a good deal of self-satisfaction in thinking you are making an impression:

and your very lack of success may even make you more
anxious that men should speak well of you. Moreover
vanity can be as apparent in face of criticism as of
approval.

'Public customs public manners breed,' and the pulpit is a very public custom, and mild clerical importance
a very common form of public manners, for, unless
the pulpit is the place where you are humblest in giving
God's message, it is certain to be the place where you are
vainest in giving your own.

The only safety is in not trying to impress at all, but
in seeking only to persuade men by enabling them to see
truth and right for themselves. Yet even in this you
will find deliverance only as it is by faith in the power of
truth and right to be its own witness, and not in your
gift of persuasion.

It may be a painfully slow business to wait on this
ministry, but is any other worth serving at all? Suppose
you could impress people, as Saul was impressed at the
evangelistic meeting at Ramoth, where he stripped off
his clothes of dignity, and lay down for a day and a
night in an agony of bitter remorse and good resolution,
what would it amount to if next day your hearers were,
as he was, ashamed of their weakness, and became the
same as before, only more so? Peter the Hermit swept
multitudes into the Crusades by the mere impression of
an oratory which was like sending round the fiery cross,
and how much did it really lift up men's souls or achieve
good in any proportion to the misery? We have seen
whole nations moved by mere impression in our time,
and it has been mostly, so far, to disregard the gentle
voice of reason and humanity.

To sweep people off their feet by religious impression
may be less immediately disastrous than by political, but
as it is emotion undirected by mind or conscience, it is
only less outwardly dangerous because it has less opportunity and is perhaps inwardly even greater disaster.
When our Lord saw it rising among His followers, He
at once crushed it, so that the multitudes went no more

after Him ; and His whole way of teaching was a demand that men should sit down and count the cost. " The spirits of the prophets are subject to the prophets, for God is not the author of confusion but of peace."

The fourth is to deliver your own souls.

Here, again, truth and error lie near together. Like the Apostle you ought to be able to say " My gospel," for unless it is good news to you, it is not likely to be to anyone else. You will only speak with authorities, and not with authority, unless the truth has already exercised dominion over your own soul. Yet to be concerned, as Parker put it, merely with getting it off your mind and not on to mine, is not preaching. And this is true of discharging your conscience as well as of unloading your mind. To some people washing their hands in public, like Pilate, is an obsession. What is called preaching for a witness is often no more, for it is concerned only with the witness being delivered, not with it being received. The preacher must lose himself in his audience and in appealing to their understanding and conscience, and short of this he does not deal aright with his subject or discharge his own obligation.

But if you are to avoid all these pitfalls, and commend yourselves to every man's conscience of truth and right alone, yet with such a comprehensive manifestation of the truth as will be fresh and convincing perhaps for a lifetime, would you not require personal quality which you are far from being assured of possessing ? And it is needless to deny how much personal quality counts. Nothing else, not even gifts of grace, can wholly take its place. When God gives some prophets, it means that He sends them with the natural endowment of insight and courage and forceful character, telling speech and intrepid action, as well as faith and peace and love ; and the weight of the message depends largely on the weight of the ambassador.

Dr Chalmers's favourite question about anyone he did not know was, " Is he a man of weight ? " No doubt this included ability, but it mainly concerned depth and force of character. Without it can anyone be truly a prophet? About all the Hebrew prophets, even if in varying degree, there could be no question : and of modern prophets we may have doubts about its possession, but none about its necessity. For any ministry, among the gifts which are a call to it, this of personal weight ought to be set in the forefront. Nothing counts so much in preaching, at least for enduring impression, nor, for that matter, in any part of a man's ministry.

Two incidents will illustrate the difference between having and wanting this personal weight.

The one was a religious address during the war. When it was done my neighbour turned and said, "Had this been reported, it would read quite well, yet our friend somehow impresses one as so small that nothing he says carries any weight."

The other was a political speech by Viscount Grey in the far-off days when he was Sir Edward, and I lived in his constituency. The local reporter said of it, " I think I have reported every word exactly. Indeed few speakers are easier to report, because there never is anything unexpected either in form or substance. Yet I know that the report will give no idea of the impression of the speech, for when Grey says it, even the most commonplace utterance seems to carry weight." Then he went on to say, " This personal weight is a very mysterious business. When I see Grey in a gathering of small tradesmen and nobodies in this small country town, never putting himself forward, but talking to everyone as his equal, I ask myself, ' Is this the man to whom all the chancelleries in Europe give heed ? ' But presently I see that everyone recognises this peculiar personal weight ; and that it would be the same anywhere. It is not his position, it is not his reputation, it is not his ability, it is somehow just the man himself."

The largest part of the answer is that this was how God has made them both. One man is six feet and the other not even five, morally as well as physically, and you cannot, by taking at least direct thought, add a cubit to either stature. Nevertheless in bad conditions you are stunted, and in good you grow bigger and stronger; and this is still more true of moral stature, and, moreover, this growth is not arrested in your teens.

Two conditions were evident in Grey, and I think that they are the essentials. The first was an intercourse with men which was made easy by not concerning himself at all about what they thought of him; and the second was a love of Nature and the quiet things of life, which never deserted him amid the worst stress and hurly-burly of public affairs. Nothing stunts the moral growth so much as vanity swayed by what others think of us, and interest only in the noisy and ephemeral.

The first requirement, then, is to live among men with an interest in all they think about everything except yourselves.

You do not respect a man as man, if you are concerned about what he thinks of yourself personally, because you are not concerned with the truth that is in him, but with the complacency. Moreover you are not truly respecting yourselves, without which you cannot truly respect anyone. Only because everyone may be a spirit which judges all things and is judged of no man should you honour him; and that is impossible if you yourself are allowing your own judgment to be swayed by man's opinion of you, and not to be determined by your own judgment of truth and right in the sight of God. This applies to all dealing with men, but specially to preaching, which cannot be of any value unless it speak to men as thus called to judge for themselves in God's sight. If you are not such men yourselves there will be no moral weight behind anything you say.

The second concerns the quiet things of life and Nature.

Matthew Arnold, in an essay on Poetry, says that the first qualification of a poet is " a serious view of life."

He finds it, as some would think strangely, in Burns;
or if they agreed it would be because they thought of
something like 'The Cottar's Saturday Night.' But
what Arnold means is that Burns is not interested in
the trappings of life, but in life itself, its common joys
and sorrows, its loves and its hopes, its aspirations and its
desires. Such was the stuff of his poetry, and his one
concern is to express it truthfully. This can be seen in
any true poet, but perhaps most in Shakespeare. He used
great names and pageantry, as in the theatre of his time,
but what interests him is just human nature in the midst
of life, and of this passionate interest in life his profound
knowledge of it is ample proof. Even a mere voice from
a crowd he makes individual and characteristic.

More even than the poet, however, this kind of
serious view of life is required in the preacher. He has
still less to do with externals, and more to do with life's
joys and sorrows, sins and triumphs, hopes and fears,
loves and hatreds. If nothing else counts for him in
comparison, he will not lack a message nor personal
weight behind it.

Yet while 'the proper study of mankind is man,' it is
not in isolation from all else. Man can only be rightly
seen against his background; and our study will have
different results as we see him against God's work or
only man's. In these days of rapid travel more people
can look upon more of the world than ever before; but
looking is not seeing. You can look upon as much of
the Lake District reclining at your ease in a motor car
in a day as Wordsworth looked upon in a lifetime on
foot, but you will not see as much of the Nature 'which
never did betray the heart that loved her' as he did
in half an hour wandering 'lonely as a cloud'; even
if you could climb among the everlasting hills, you
would be making too much row to hear its silence;
if you ever noticed the rainbow, your head would be
too much puzzled to know how so silently it kept pace
with your rapid motion, for your heart to leap up at its
glory; and you would find less of the thoughts that lie

too deep for tears from the whole panorama than he did
from the ' meanest flower that blows.'

Yet Nature also is not best seen by itself.   Mere Nature
description seldom rises to poetry.   Deep insight into
Nature requires a serious view of life ; and a serious view
of life is maintained in serenity by insight into Nature.
Hence the true poet all the more describes Nature with
accuracy as well as beauty that he sees it as the setting
of humanity.

May it not be that the present rush and flurry of life,
with its wasteful flying from one interest to another
without ever exhausting any, is largely from seeing man
against the noisy and garish background of man's manu-
facturing and not against the quiet, gracious, changing,
yet abiding beauty of God's creating ?   Is this not why
man's weight for any enterprise he takes in hand is so
small ?   Is it because God is making men of lighter
weight, that no one seems in our day to be producing
anything that has spiritual greatness ; or is it that men
live in a glare of light and a blare of noise, without
reflecting from the unruffled surface of their souls the
quiet, serene procession of the sun and the stars and
breathing the bracing atmosphere of spring, summer,
autumn and winter, in healing fellowship with mother
earth, which feeds their spirits as well as their bodies
by a bounty which is as free from self-advertising as it is
from stint ?

A young woman said to an old friend, " I have the
liveliest interest in reading—" mentioning half a dozen
novelists who are already forgotten " but I find the Bible
extremely dull."   " My dear," my friend replied, " I
have the deepest sympathy with you.   The other night
I went to the cinema.   There was a most glorious racket.
Trains whizzed past, people escaped from windows,
there was no end of a hue and cry ; and I was enormously
interested.   When I came out it was a lovely night,
with the moon and the stars shining bright above me ;
and I was not interested a bit.   But I wonder if I could
give you any idea of the vision that once flashed its

splendour on me, when, about your own age, I read
these simple words :

> The moon doth with delight
> Look round her when the heavens are bare ;
> Waters on a starry night
> Are beautiful and fair."

I should like you to ponder this saying of Conrad, "And
the unwearied self-forgetful attention to every phase of
the living universe reflected in our consciousness may
be our appointed task on earth, a task in which fate has
engaged nothing of us except our conscience, gifted with
a voice in order to bear true testimony to the visible
wonder, the haunting terror, the infinite passion and
the illimitable serenity, to the supreme law and abiding
mystery of the sublime spectacle."

This is not everything if you are to help towards
making better men and a better world. Yet, even for
this end, it has a much larger place than is generally
accorded it. Is the restless desire to amend everything
in accord with some hastily conceived ideal, which is
often no more than acceptance of the impatient, shallow
thinking floating in the atmosphere around, without
insight, without appreciation, without love of anything,
really God's patient way with this imperfect world ?
Is not the better way first to appreciate and then to
manifest the best we can discover of God's truth in the
quiet, beautiful, enduring elements of Nature and human
nature ?   Would it not at once give you a message, and
quiet weight and strength behind it ?

At the same time there are diversities of gifts, and not
least of personal weight, and if God has given it you in
large measure, few gifts will make your ministry easier.

A great example is Isaiah. He lived in a less calamitous time than Jeremiah, and his message was not so
immediately of ruin. Yet his calmer march through life
than Jeremiah's was due less to circumstances than to
the man himself.

No doubt circumstances counted. Jeremiah, as a

country priest, the son of a country priest, could not speak with the enemy in the gate as an aristocrat, like Isaiah, who was probably of royal blood. Isaiah, too, had a wider outlook, could speak of public affairs with more knowledge and experience, and could express himself with a sublimity and an irony which was not easy to counter. When he called the world alliances for attack ' smoking stumps of firebrands,' and the alliances for defence ' trusting the braggart that sits still,' they were shots between wind and water. But above all he was a born leader, and gathered round him a remnant of loyal followers, and was more indifferent naturally to what men thought of him than a sensitive nature like Jeremiah's could be. Wherefore he could dwell calmly in spirit by the waters of Shiloah that go softly, and could sing a song of the beloved concerning his vineyard, and speak of his wife as the prophetess, and the children that God had given him as for signs and for wonders : whereas Jeremiah was a lonely man and the one prophet who seldom uses illustrations from Nature.

At the same time the account sometimes given of Isaiah, as if his power lay in being a supremely able and astute politician, is wholly misleading. He was a prophet who judged what is expedient by what is right, and not a politician who judged right by what is expedient. His whole mind was set on knowing what was God's mind in the business, not man's.

Wherefore, in spite of his great natural weight, in the end his power was faith, not mere native force. It was because God had taken him with a strong hand that he did not fear man's fears. He did not make haste, rushing hither and thither after human devices for safety, because he believed in God above all and in all. He could keep to inward peace and purity and outward consideration and justice between man and man, because he believed that God was in them.

Yet for you there is perhaps still more to learn from Jeremiah, with his humble position, his sensitive nature, which felt bitterly his alienation from his fellows and their fierce hostility to himself as well as to his message. Though naturally more fearful, more sensitive, even more hesitating in his faith, his more terrible message he continued to deliver to the end ; and, through a still more calamitous time, he stood faithful amid the faithless.

Wherefore, though you should be grateful for any gift that enables you to do your work easily, the great concern is not to be able to do it easily, but to be enabled to carry it through in spite of your inward fears and outward conflicts—in short, to be able to do it at all. Just because Jeremiah did not do it easily he has an unrivalled appeal to the hearts of most of us.

And what is more, just because it drove him utterly back upon God, he gave the faith of Israel a humble, personal, purely religious quality which brought God nearer to human souls and human lives as no other prophet before or after him. In a tenderer, humbler, more simply human and religious way, he learned that no sense of human weakness and infirmity could hinder him from being able to pull down and to build up, to be as a defenced city and an iron pillar and brazen walls against the whole land and the highest therein. This was a supreme accounting of himself, but by a sufficiency that was of God.

About few things is it possible to talk more spaciously with greater unreality. You are not expecting so high and perilous a ministry in so catastrophic a time, nor are you really looking for such revolutionary results. And while in these uncertain days you never know what may be required, you are not to consider your calling more heroic than it is. It may even be very tame and safe. Then, as no life can be tame if moved by the highest interests, or safe if set on the noblest purposes, the great peril may be yours of never venturing out of shelter. Wherefore there is no ministry, the least challenging perhaps most of all, for which even the greatest natural endowment is enough, and from which you should not shrink unless you can account of yourself for it from a higher source. Even in these days of perplexity, and though you know yourselves to be quite ordinary persons, if this source of your strength is a reality and no mere pious phraseology, you can go forward with a strong hand and a stout heart to all that may be before you, and, above all, expect to have a message that will both pull down and build up.

Nevertheless it is still an accounting of yourselves, and not mere resignation either of yourselves or your work into God's hands. He does not work the willing and the doing without your working out your own salvation. Even if with fear and trembling, it is still the assurance that what you ought to do you can do, or at least that to attempt it is of more profit to the world, as well as to your own soul, than any lower aim. The best work requires vision and inspiration and power beyond your own, and these are from above. But where you have a right to expect them is at the end of your dealing with what is here below, after you have loved God and your neighbour in the practical way of giving such mind as you have to your problems, such heart as you have to men's sorrows and failures, and such strength as you have to God's service. You can look for wisdom, insight, power not your own, then and not before, yet, even then, only as sufficiency to account of yourselves equal to the task before you. Wherefore it is still one with making yourselves as efficient as you know how. God does not take your tasks off your hands and do them for you, any more than He gives you guidance without the use of your own judgment, like the Delphic oracle. We become big enough for them by attaining to full-grown manhood, but this we attain by undertaking big tasks.

Wherefore it is to be wrought for, not simply prayed for. By dealing truly in love, not in speech only, but in all things, we grow up in all things unto Him who is the head. Though this is not your weight, it is putting all the weight you have into serving the highest you know in love, which means in insight, for love alone can truly see man's heart, man's life, and God's world around him, material and spiritual, as it truly is.

You must account of yourselves for any task that comes to your hand, and no task worth doing can be faced without accounting of yourselves highly. All-sufficient weight for the task is of faith in God, not confidence in yourselves, yet as God works through us and not merely for us, you cannot be small men and do great work. Nor if you do really great work by God's help, will you remain small men. This is of faith and not of mere nature, but faith is just what enables us to be utterly loyal to truth, because God and truth and reality are one, and to trust wholly in love because He is love, and no other might in the end rules the world. Before you nothing lower is set than the measure of the stature of Jesus Christ.

How supreme this is we can see by comparing it with so great a man as Paul, and finding that even he is right in thinking he had not attained and was not yet full grown.

In my student days there was a German professor who used to interrupt his enthusiastic exposition of the Apostle with the interjection, " Aber, meine Herren, dieser Paulus war ein feiner Kerl." He was a fine fellow, and to know it is worth reams of exposition for genuine understanding. Besides his courage, intellectual, moral, and physical, there is his gift of sympathy and friendship, and large-hearted humanity. Yet he is not delivered so utterly from striving as his Master ; he could not have sat at meat with the same gracious influence among publicans and outcasts ; he could not burn so clearly his own smoke ; he could not find the same quiet enlargement of spirit with his Father alone on the mountain under the silent stars ; he had not the same insight either into Nature or human nature ; his thoughts about God and His doings he could not set free from all abstractions, and make a simple, gracious, self-revealing light, shining upon the common earth and the simple ways of simple men, like his Lord.

We are all a very long way from this fulness of stature, but you are ambassadors on His behalf, not your own, and something of this convincing weight of truth, lived as well as spoken, you may be enabled to make felt in all you say in His name.   You may to the end have still more reason than the Apostle to say you have not attained, but at least you can, with him, as long as life lasts, forget the things that are behind and press forward to those that are before.

VIII

FIXED CONVICTION AND UNCHANGING TRUTH

G REAT as the significance of the man himself may be for his work, even weight and faith will not make a preacher a lasting power without a message which is at once great enough to claim attention and varied enough to maintain it. This involves two seeming opposites, which we shall call fixity of conviction and variety of mood.

As fixity of conviction is of value only as it is from the vision of unchanging truth, it is akin to our last subject. Therefore with it we begin. It has to do not only with faith, but with the objects of faith, not only with believing in God, but with what we believe about Him ; and it ought to be what the Apostle calls ' zeal according to knowledge.'

While he does not praise a zeal that is not according to knowledge, he recognises its power. Zeal of any quality is a force, and highly infectious. Nor may it be less so or less assured of being of God for being negative, denunciatory, traditional, partisan, bitter—in short, everything that is not of God's true mind. Nay, the cruder it is, the more of the letter and less of the spirit, the more of vehemence and less of persuasion, even the more material, the more effective it may be, at least for a time, as the Apostle himself had good cause to know. Israel which had Abraham to its father according to the flesh, was easier to distinguish and more readily evolved enthusiasm than the spiritual Israel which was according to his faith ; obedience to every word of the Old Testament was plain and decisive, compared with seeing in it the growing manifestation of a rule of God by writing His law on the heart, which made many of its ordinances only temporary devices, and seemed to leave Scripture at the mercy of man's picking and choosing; circumcision in the flesh required only the eyes of the body, circumcision of the heart required the insight of the soul. No wonder that Paul was looked upon as a renegade, and that, for a long time, he seemed to be fighting a losing battle. Perhaps he has not yet won as much as is assumed, for while the immediate form of this zeal changed, zeal for subjection to the letter against the liberty of the spirit, for ritual precept against the righteousness of the renewed heart, for the visible institution against the fellowship of the spirit is the same in substance, and did not end with the Judaisers. To this day zeal for them abides in power, confident of being the only zeal for God that knows no vagueness and no compromise. Truth which is its own witness and appeals only to knowledge, seems to be merely man's device, which, lacking the imperious authority of Bible or Church and not backed by a very material heaven and hell, is thought to be weak, and the cause of all the Church's weakness, and in particular to make its preaching uncertain and of no authority.

Nor is it merely that zeal may be intense in inverse ratio to spiritual vision. It may also be in inverse ratio to any kind of importance in its object. Tithing mint and anise and cummin may still stir it more than the weightier matters of the law, and the living word of God be still made of none effect by detailed and frivolous and even meaningless traditions. Compared with the great and vital problems of faith and action facing the Church, most ecclesiastical discussions are about fringes and phylacteries. Much of it is due to the fear that God cannot look after His own truth, but has to depend for its defence on human regulations. Hence, as it has been expressed, we have the defence of religion by every argument except religion itself, and the one person not expected to look after it is God.

All zeal is contagious, but if a real positive conviction is backed by suavity and resource it is still more effective.

An acquaintance was an Individualist of this ardent type. His zeal, which burned not with mere flame but like the heart of a furnace, had a quite amazing power of drawing in everything to feed it. To the hasty observer it had the mere negative form that no government can ever be more than Bumble, whose job is to keep some kind of decent order, and who, when he attempts to go beyond and meddles with matters like religion, education and economics, can only deal out the thinnest kind of skilly. But this negation was inspired by passionate agreement with Barbour—

> Ah! freedom is a noble thing,
> Freedom all solace to man gives;
> He lives at ease that freely lives.

You could meet him anywhere, under any circumstances, and in five minutes, quite naturally and without in the least forcing the conversation, he would be in the heart of the subject. You might roll him in the dust in argument, and he was not in the least disconcerted. He did not wish to humble you in debate and did not mind being humbled himself. His business was to enable you to see the vision which inspired his own soul, and this he did with quietness, unfailing courtesy, endless resource. Supposing you had zeal, thus inspired and with this self-forgetting courtesy and resource, for the vision of a still higher freedom in the rule of God, could any limit be set either to the efficacy or the endurance of your advocacy?

All zeal is of power, but only enlightened zeal is of profit. While the Apostle recognises the power of any kind of conscientious zeal, he is not approving of it. Conscientiousness does not end with zeal for what we think right. Its higher exercise is to discover what is truly right. Even a zeal for God is not admirable unless it is according to knowledge of what God really approves and really purposes. Nor is it justified even by what is right, if this is only by accident and not discernment. Knowledge, as the Apostle meant it,

F

must be your own, and may not be merely formal rules laid down for you, or infection by the zeal of others, or impression from the ancient and accepted.

I have seen too much of the early success of opinions accepted ready-made and of the faltering accents of those who would only speak what they do know, to promise you immediate or possibly ultimate popularity, if you choose this way.   There is an American saying, that a lie has gone a league while truth is putting on its boots.   And if you have to make your own boots, the person who is content to put on other people's will have a still longer start.   Though you will never arrive at what may be a distant end without limping, except in your own, if your zeal is thus limited to your knowledge, it may never swell the numbers of your congregation, and though it make them a leaven amid the society in which they live and work, will it not be a small leaven?

While you cannot regard blind tradition as a real conviction of God's word, all that is left you in these days of historical research, with its criticism both of Scripture and dogma, may seem too cold and meagre and bare to give the old note of authority in your preaching.   With this loss has it not lost much of the old impressiveness?   And, for good or ill, there is a sense, and a very important sense, in which it has.

The typical Highlander is far more of a born Catholic than the most High Church Anglican.   To question a word of Scripture or touch the smallest brick in the accepted system of dogma is to bring down the whole edifice of religion about your ears.   I once had the privilege of discussing his position with one of the ablest and best of old Highland ministers, and then of hearing him preach.   He listened to my views with great patience ; and, so far from denouncing them, recognised that if I had entered on this road of receiving only what, with reverent study and thought, I took to be according to knowledge, I must tread it to the end. " But," he added, " what would a Highlander like me do without authority ? "   Then I listened to his preaching, and it was, perhaps, the most impressive utterance I ever heard. A striking, dignified, patriarchal figure, such as we do not seem to be able to produce in our restless days ; a clear, carrying, moving voice, with a natural but restrained eloquence ; a glow of imagination and a felicity and lucidity of style ; and, like an ancient prophet, all enforced with " Thus saith the Lord." I felt not only the poverty of my own utterance in comparison, but that something rich and strong had been lost to our age.

Yet as he went on I realised that he was not speaking, like Jesus, with authority, but, like the scribes, with authorities. It was "Thus saith the Lord," not because the Lord had taken him with a strong hand and said, " Thou shalt not fear their fear," but because it was in the Bible and the Creed, and the fear of departing from them was heavy upon his soul. He was offering a proclamation to be submitted to, not good news to be received because it had won the heart. There was nothing of seeing in a glass darkly, but all was formulated dogma, which could never have found its way into parables about the common world of men.

Here is the difference between speaking with authorities and speaking with authority. The former speaks from what God has said and done in the past ; the latter, even if from the revealed, is from it as the revealing, as valid for us now as it ever was in the past. The only true authority is God's truth itself and its own witness to itself ; and you speak with its authority only when you speak that which you know and testify that which you have seen. To persuade men to receive it as their own you must be able to say with the Apostle, " My good news." Paul once or twice quotes Jesus as supporting his own view, but he never uses even His authority to say, " Take this, whether you see it or not." Instead, Jesus is always to him the supreme way of seeing for ourselves God's mind and God's way of working.

When we go to the Gospels, we find Jesus saying,

" Moses said unto you, but I say unto you," yet not as a new and greater legislation. Moses, He said, considered the hardness of men's hearts, but I appeal to what is deeper, tenderer, more truly God's image. "He that is taught of God comes to Me," and knows of himself My teaching. Jesus is the supreme authority in religion precisely because He never spoke merely as an authority, but always said, "You will see this to be true, unless you blind your eyes by hypocrisy." Hypocrisy alone He recognised as the one fatal barrier, not because it is a specially malignant sin, but because it is not open to the witness of truth. He required only one condition. "He that willeth to do the will of God shall know the teaching."

Here another question arises. May there not be great truths you do not know, great visions you have not seen, great experiences you have not undergone; and may not this limit and impoverish your ministry?

But while you should speak only from your own knowledge, this does not mean that you must speak only from your own experience. Your own experience should be enriched by the whole experience of the saints, and you may speak of it as theirs, while it is still only by some dim understanding and appreciation your own.

Even when this is in Scripture, it should be of your own first-hand knowledge. By this I mean through like experience, not mere learning. Nevertheless, first-hand knowledge even as learning is a good foundation. As the Scriptures are ancient documents you must read books about them, but you should have such first-hand knowledge as enables you to judge for yourselves what the writers of the Scriptures really mean, and not the meaning imposed upon them. You must know what they themselves thought and the time to which they addressed it, before you can discover what value it has for ours. Similarly with the history of the Church, you must seek to get behind dates and creeds and events to the life which wrought through them, and you will not understand if you confine your attention to the religious and omit the secular. In the end you need some kind of theology, a view of God and man and the world, as seen in the light of Jesus Christ. This is not necessarily what you can formulate, and it should never find its way into your preaching as mere theology. But it will be a bigger theology if you do first-hand reading of those who have thought most deeply on the subject.

In your present studies it is not possible that you should gain such knowledge of all or perhaps any of them, and much less of all the Cosmologies, Anthropologies, Comparative Religions, Psychologies, Sociologies and several other profundities which are supposed to be necessary for the ministerial calling. You can acquire them all at third-hand from lectures or little handbooks which are second-hand, and have all the pride of the schoolgirl who knew not what the astronomer did with his time as she had learnt the whole of astronomy last term. Knowledge of one subject—knowledge on which you can exercise your own judgment—is in comparison a slow and drab business. But if you have mastered one subject from the foundation, you will be able to acquire anything else you need to know. And, considering the uncertainty of what may meet you in this varied life and changing age, this is the sole possible equipment. Ready-made provision for all emergencies would require omniscience, and not the purblind foresight of even the wisest teacher. Moreover, if you ever come to be in a position where the Sociology or any of the rest thus superficially acquired might seem to be applicable, you would not only have to learn it anew from life, but have all the trouble of unlearning first what you thought you knew.

The question is whether you want wearing or showy material, or to use another metaphor, whether you want to kindle bonfires in your youth or to keep a spark alive on the hearthstone to old age. Knowledge laboriously acquired at first-hand is not very combustible material for setting zeal ablaze. But whether this is to profit or not depends on what should be the object of the zeal, and on what you mean by conviction. Zeal which is smoke and flame is a great power for a finality you can cram down people's throats, but the clear shining of a steady light is needed for the infinite truth of God, regarding which it is the greatest of all successes to stir people by your example and your teaching to hunger and thirst after it.

If your own vision of it is growing and this increasingly inspires your preaching, so that Sunday by Sunday your people see more clearly the gracious significance of the God and Father of our Lord Jesus Christ for the meaning of the world and the value of the human soul, and go more cheerfully, hopefully and courageously about the work of their daily lives, your ministry will grow with the years, while cleverness, ability, eloquence, without this inspiration, ever wane in power.

To attempt to command dogmatic assurance would be mere hopeless insincerity, whereas it is just humble sincerity, asking the way to Zion with the face thitherward, that persuades people to gird up their loins and follow. The right fixity of conviction is not in remaining always the same. It is truth, not your conviction of it, that is unchanging. What should never change is setting truth always before you and following it with all your mind and heart and strength.

Consistency has been called the virtue of small minds ; and, if it is mere concern to show that we never change, it certainly marks an arrested mind. Yet to be ' everything by turns and nothing long ' is quite as certainly not the way to make a deep, lasting and increasing impression. It should be like Paul's change of his plan to visit once again the church at Corinth. His opponents called it mere fickleness, but the Apostle said it was not swithering between yea and nay, but was his Master's Yea and his own Amen. Plans he might make, but they were only for the end of the fullest service of God's good news in Jesus Christ : and if altered circumstances, with more immediate and urgent calls, met him, it was the highest consistency to set aside his own plans. So with your own convictions. If you are growing, they will change, possibly towards what may seem a quite opposite direction. Yet, like tacking with a changing wind, it should be plain that the port you are making for is still the same. Throughout there should be the deeper consistency of seeking only to know God's truth and following only His purpose. Moreover, while you may, as you go on, have to correct some points in your bearings, this goal is not anywhere on the wide horizon, but there will be the further consistency that you are still advancing in a course that is never far from the same direction. Your compasses may need to be corrected, yet you still know that the Pole Star is the true North.

IX

CHANGING MOOD AND LIFE'S VARIETY

A CONVICTION is not a mere idea to be spoken of once, then, like a *bon-mot*, never to be repeated, at least in the same company. It is shown to be a conviction by what has been described as 'recurrences and fervours.' If it is a central conviction, you will in a sense be saying it always, and if it is about what is truly central, you ought to be saying it always or there will be no continuity of persuasion or increase of interest.

In the *Autocrat of the Breakfast Table*, Wendell Holmes says, "What would Socrates have made out of 'Know thyself' if he had said it only once?" In his own time people said to him, "You are always saying the same thing"; and Socrates replied, "If I am asked what is twice two, am I not always to say the same thing?" Straining after variety as mere hearing or telling some new thing, even if it were that twice two are five, arrives nowhere.

Think also of the reiteration in Paul's account of his own life-work. "Wherefore, O king Agrippa, I was not disobedient to the heavenly vision." With this opening you expect to hear of something new and wonderful. But instead, he goes on to say, "I showed first unto them at Damascus and at Jerusalem and throughout all the coasts of Judea and then to the Gentiles, that they should repent and turn to God and do works meet for repentance."

Nothing, it might be thought, could be more monotonous, and 'Know thyself' and 'Repent and amend' would have been sheer commonplace moral platitudes had they been mere catchwords and not obedience to a heavenly vision of the tremendous issues, for time and eternity, involved in them.

Great, nevertheless, is the power of catchwords. Dr Johnson speaks of people who, like dogs, bark at a word. Hence the influence even of unproved assertion, if it is said confidently enough and emphatically enough, and is taken up and repeated by many voices. The very uniformity of utterance adds to its efficacy. When it becomes a slogan, it can rule whole nations, at least for a time. Even our own rather slow and stolid people have not been immune. When ' A war to end war ' was the slogan how much attention was given to those who said ' Wars only breed wars '? And when ' A country fit for heroes ' took its place, the suggestion that it might mean ' a country fit only for heroes,' seemed desecration of the sanctuary.

In no sphere can assertion be so effective as in religion, or familiar exalted phrases gather round them such a numinous atmosphere, till they become like that ' blessed word Mesopotamia.' Even expressions which should have a profound meaning, like ' atonement ' and ' accepting Christ ' and ' justification by faith,' may come to be mere unctuous phraseology. If you ever take a service where the members of the audience express their outspoken approval in pious ejaculations, you will discover how much it is evoked by familiar phrases, and silenced by what requires meditation. Even where custom prescribes silence many never feel edified unless they have a liberal dose of numinous, familiar phraseology. They would be shocked to be told that they are ritualists, but it is just ritual, and, as much as visible forms, may be a way of speaking so that people may not understand. In spite of its familiarity it is the ten thousand words in an unknown tongue.

Coleridge says that it is the work of genius to restore what is tarnished by use to its first uncommon lustre. And perhaps it is one of the first and most difficult tasks of the preacher to restore the original lustre to well-worn Scripture phrases. This requires digging down,

not only to the eternal divine meaning in them, but also
to the significance of it for the common ways of human
life.   It is at once uncovering the foundation and showing
that all mortal concerns can be built on it.

Socrates was able to go on saying " Know thyself,"
because he saw in this knowledge a wisdom which
reached up to the highest truth and down to the
humblest duties. Paul was able to go on preaching
that men should repent, because it was at once turning
to God and transforming life in its everyday thoughts
and actions.

Here is the difference between the commonplace
and what we may call the elemental. By this I mean
what has abiding working significance in human life.
So long as what you say is aglow with the sense of the
overwhelming importance of man's endeavours and
failures, hopes and discouragements, aspiration after
good, and complacency with attainment, unsatisfied
spiritual longings, and comfortable satisfaction with
material success, you will not escape the need for
repetition and insistence, and it will not descend to the
merely commonplace. Without it preaching is only
a variety-show which, though it may commend itself
for a time to an age that has been described as ' the age
of snippets,' an age which sacrifices coherent principle
and practice to constant change of interest and application, will not be to lasting edification, or even as an
entertainment long compete with the many livelier
forms of it now so accessible to all.

Yet even the highest aim may not save it from becoming monotonous. Unfortunately there is no warning so
monotonous as the need for it : but, unfortunately also,
it is worthless when it becomes monotonous. Nor will
you escape by mere shrillness. The noisiest bell, if it
sound evenly, can become a lullaby. And even a true
and vital sense of the elemental can become mere
shrillness. Unless it respond in varying tone to the
many chords, both of harmony and discord, which the
manifold experiences of life evoke in the human heart,

it will not continue to be heard except with the outward ear.

If you read a little about Socrates in the *Dialogues* of Plato and about Paul in his Epistles, you will find the true reason why they could go on effectively saying the same thing. Socrates arguing with young men in the market-place is gay and friendly and subtle, and a master of illustrations from common things, but in *The Apology* he strikes a very different note and rises to very different heights. Compare the passionate defence of Christian liberty in the Epistle to the Galatians, with the reasoned defence of Romans, and the calm appeal to show our moderation to all men in Philippians. Take even one Epistle, say 1 Corinthians, and consider what a range of changing tone and emotion there is in its plain practical dealing with difficult situations, and its glowing poetry on love and immortality. If with this varied response to the variety of life's experience, you can say, " This is undeniable eternal truth, vital for your common everyday life and practice," and can touch men's changing moods thereby, you can go on repeating as much as you like. When this is wanting, all the capacity and cleverness in the world will not save your preaching from being rather a dull amusement, for which the cinema and the music-hall will be much more effective substitutes. Just as any kind of fixity of zeal is infectious, any kind of variety of mood is appealing.

A very bright young woman made this defence of one who had given offence by saying what was more plain than pleasant. " You can't help being interested in what the creature says, for he has such a flair for life's variety that you never know what mood he will be in ; and you should not take offence, for he is not finding fault, but only saying what he thinks to be true : and he would say it as coolly to Solomon or the Queen of Sheba as to you."

Here are the essential points. The first is that the moods should respond to life's variety, not to the state of your digestion ; the second, that they are from objective interests, not your own sentimentality ; the third, that they are subordinated to truth, without fear or favour. This last is of supreme importance. Much will be forgiven—even not very wise utterance —to a person who has the courage of his convictions and says only what he thinks true and right, as it appeals to him, and without personal feeling. While there may be warm feeling, it must be cool courage, for, while you should put as much warmth into what you say as is in you, the same thing said in mere hot temper will only increase irritation and diminish persuasiveness.

Temper is not a mood in the sense I mean. Indignation may be : and I am far from wishing to say that you should never be stirred even to hot indignation, or that you are never to give it utterance. But make sure that it is really indignation against wrong, and not temper stirred by touchiness. On all matters merely affecting yourself take Lord Beaconsfield's advice to public men : " Never complain and never explain." More particularly, never do it from the pulpit, where no one has a chance of replying. But, also, never do it by letter, which, too, is a coward's refuge. It will never do any good, and the plainest words can be twisted to a quite opposite meaning. If you must deal with anything wrong between you and another person, take the advice of the Master to have it out between you and him alone.

Even when you have right indignation do not rush into the pulpit with it in its first fermentation, any more than you should rush into the press.

The Goths used to discuss their plans, first, when they were drunk that they might not lack boldness, and again, when they were sober, that their boldness should be qualified by prudence. While you will not resort to such extraneous aid, do not forget that there are other intoxicants than spirituous liquors which may carry you along, and possibly too far.

Whatever you do about other matters, write with meticulous care anything you have to say which may have any suggestion of upbraiding. Write it first when your indignation is hot upon you by all means. But then lay it aside for a season till you can read it again in cold blood. Then you will probably bring it to the proper temperature.

A mood of fault-finding is, above all, to be shunned. It was said in Scotland in former days that when an Established Church minister turned lazy he took to preaching his old sermons, and his Free Church brother, in like case, took to scolding his congregation. The use of old sermons for no better reason than laziness is likely to be *cramben bis coctam*, which, translated into northern vernacular, is 'cauld kail het again'; and is not even likely to be well heated. Yet it is more tolerable than the other device of disguising the ancient flavour with vinegar.

An old lady who had been visiting her married daughter in another place was telling how happy her daughter was in her life generally. "But," she added, " there is one thing I am very distressed about. Neither she nor her husband can abide their minister's preaching. In some ways it is real good preaching, but it is full of telling folks their faults. It may be good to be told our faults occasionally, but we none of us like to hear nothing else, and it depends on how it is done. Nathan, when he went to tell David his fault, had a parable, and Mr Smith is not a good hand at the parable."

If you must find fault, don't forget the parable, and if you have to find a new one for it every time, you are not likely to do it too often, and by the time you have put it into that shape, it will no longer be in a mere mood of scolding.

But sameness of mood, even the sweetest, becomes a weariness. Cream is a name for all that is delectable, but as a constant sauce it would be worse than constant curry; nor is constant cheerfulness much better. A person with a smile glued on his face and hilariousness always ringing in his voice is only a little less trying than the knight of the rueful countenance and gloomy utterance.

> Thou'rt such a testy, touchy, pleasant fellow,
> With something grave and gay and mellow,
> Hast so much wit and mirth and spleen about thee
> There is no living with thee or without thee.

This is a little overdoing it, yet for sustaining interest, even mere mood, changing, like our weather, in one day from sunshine to shade, from summer to winter, can go a long way. There was a preacher whom a friend described as ' an ecclesiastical Micawber.' On Saturday he wrote you that, " Hope had sunk beneath the horizon, and the undersigned is crushed." You called round on Monday to commiserate with him, and you found that ' the cloud had passed from the dreary scene, and the god of day is once more high upon the mountain-tops, and my foot upon its native heath.' He would be possessed by an idea which dominated him, like Mr Micawber's expectation of something turning up, and he would preach on it for weeks. But it touched him, and he was able to touch his hearers with such unexpected variety of mood that few realised how much, merely intellectually considered, it was only one idea, and that perhaps not of overwhelming importance. In consequence, the interest of an audience, more than usually interested in new ideas, never flagged.

I am not setting Mr Micawber up as a pattern to follow. You should have your moods in hand as well as your temper. As George Herbert says :

> Who keeps not guard upon himself is slack
> And rots to nothing at the next great thaw :
> Man is a shop of rules ; a well-trussed pack,
> Whose every parcel underwrites a law.
> Lose not thyself nor give thy humours way :
> God gave them to thee under lock and key.

At the same time, as no one has much drive in him who has no temper to keep in hand, so no one has much scope in preaching who has no moods to keep in hand.

Nothing is so monotonous as sameness of mood. Even the most eupeptic cheerfulness can become a weariness to the flesh, which has its own distresses, and still more to the spirit, which may be passing through the deeps. A preacher who was rumoured to write in the margin of his sermons ' Weep here,' would have been no less depressing in the long run had it been ' Beam here.' Mark Tapley as a preacher would soon have been as tiresome as Mrs Gummidge, and to many even more dejecting.

Levity is not a fitting mood in preaching in any circumstances, but when a young parson in France used to talk to men just out of the trenches as if life were a gay affair, its conflicts only a football scrimmage, with a copious use of slang, the cheaper that it was mainly the clever college article, it was somewhat of an outrage. Nevertheless, to have exchanged him for Chaucer's ' full solempne man ' who speaks in one deep sombre tone, as though only the sob of the wind across a grey plateau were God's voice, and never the zephyr in the smiling valley or the tempest on shining mountain-tops, would not have won a better or more sympathetic hearing, even amid a welter of mud and sudden death.

Against two serious moods, especially, you are to be on your guard. The first is the moralistic, which is the danger of your youth ; and the second is the depressed, which may be the danger of your later years.

I once had a class of ragamuffins which, unlike most audiences, swelled in proportion to the badness of the weather. To any question asked they had one ready answer, " We must be good."

In a sense this is the whole purport of preaching ; and you are not to seek variety by diverting it to any other end. All the beauty of the human frame is stretched on one kind of skeleton, and art may not forget that to it is due the strength and poise of the human figure. But if it paint anatomy, and does not make what it knows of the subject shine through the body that is clothed upon it and the living interests which speak through the body, it is not art. Again, think of what nature makes of the golden brown tints of autumn. Only it must not lack gold, without which brown is only a dull sort of sepia. In the same way, even the call to repentance must not lack the gold of the heavenly vision of goodness and mercy.

Moreover, this vision has as its end a goodness God alone has, and is not merely doing good deeds, and still less, merely refraining from bad ones. Understanding the term mainly in this last sense, we use it freely, especially of the departed. But in the New Testament Barnabas is the only person ever spoken of, even in a less exalted sense, as a good man. How much it meant is seen by what Paul says of the good compared with the righteous. It may possibly be Barnabas also that he is thinking of, but in any case goodness was obviously taken to be an ideal far beyond mere moral insistence.

On the other hand, while we should hesitate to call anyone a saint, Paul uses it of all kinds of people who, on the lowest estimate, were not good. The reason was that saint, for him, was not one who had attained, but one who, being open to the leading of the Spirit of God, was in the way of attaining. If you bear this distinction in mind, and realise that your business is with saints directly, and only with good men indirectly, you will be delivered from the danger of becoming a mere carping conscience with its standardised morality and subtle sense of superiority, by learning that, though to everyone there is the same Spirit, there are diversities of gifts to each, and the same Lord, but diversities of administrations according to different characters, and the same God, but diversities of operations according to different circumstances, in the world where He works all in all, and that if men are open to the Spirit, directed by the Lord and right with Him who works in all and by all, they are in better hands than yours or any other mortal's, whatever be his wisdom or experience, or whatsoever authority empowers him to be a director of souls.

I trust I shall never lack sympathy even with the impatience of youth, and I am far from wishing to have your hope of changing men from what they are into what they ought to be, burdened by the discouragements and disenchantments which life has imposed upon your seniors. Yet the same discouragement and disenchantment await you if you think you can order a new character like a new suit of clothes and a new world like a new suite of offices. The wisest of us do not know the depths and heights of the human soul, and still less the manifold wisdom of God in dealing with it. But we can be learning, if we are kind and patient and have understanding of what is attempted as well as done, aspired after as well as attained.

Mere moral preaching is apt to be an exaltation of the man of well-drilled habits and firm-knit will, who is too cold to be tempted and too self-possessed to be taken unaware, and a despising of the little one, who is sensitive with the distress of many failures and is only struggling out of bad influences and evil habits, and that not always victoriously, yet is redeemed by some little faith and hope and love in the inmost heart. When our Lord says that it is the greatest angels, those who stand closest to the heavenly Father, who are the guardian angels of such little ones, He is expressing a judgment, not only of God's care in proportion to human need, but also of what God cares for as most precious in His sight.

It is doing Christ's words and not merely hearing them which is building on the rock. Yet His words are not mere moral preaching, much less moralistic preaching—preaching merely concerned with getting certain things done, for God looks on the heart, not the outward appearance, and with Him the faith of the heart is one with moral reality. The supreme quality of the teaching of Jesus is that in it morality is religion and religion morality, and with nothing which does not at

G

once reach up to God and down to every trial and task of life. That is your ideal. It is to lead men to God, that there they should find their true and varied selves in right bearing of the trials He appoints, as in the most active service He requires. Yet God's will is not truly accepted merely by grinning and setting the teeth. Righteousness is not by that kind of law, but is genuine righteousness only when accepted joyously as the one blessed guide to all life's gracious uses.

The burden of the Lord, not in the old sense of an oracle, but in the sense of a load, is nearer what it is in many minds; and much preaching gives the impression that goodness is very dreary, and only to be endured in the fear of where the bypaths of evil end and the happier prospects in this respect of keeping to the beaten track.

Yet without God's requirements as the security of His order, there would be little joy in the world: for on His order depend the beautiful, the gracious, the self-forgetting, the themes of all great poetry and song. The question for you also is how to turn life's tasks and trials from a dirge to a song, that doubtless has a plaintive undertone of failure but rises also with triumphant note of hope and gladness.

The other danger is the mood of fixed dejection, or if it be short of this, a kind of drab greyness, which is like what a native, who returned to it after sojourning in sunnier lands, said of the climate of Manchester, " The same old thing, neither summer nor winter, but all back-end." String after string breaks in the violin, and as there is no Paganini to play on what is left, it becomes a mere wailing note.

The most wonderful example of the opposite is our Lord's teaching. Take His treatment of hypocrisy. " Woe unto you, Pharisees." This is not denunciation but a lament in an Old Testament form over the inevitable consequences of evil. Yet with what terrible precision it is justified. " Ye devour widows' houses, and for a pretence make long prayers." And how awful is the judgment that such doings cannot escape. " Ye serpents, ye generation of vipers, how can ye escape the damnation of hell ? "   How changed is the tone when He comes to speak of the misery the evil works for him who does it, how thrilling the poignancy of the sorrow : " O Jerusalem, Jerusalem, which killest the prophets, and stonest them that are sent unto thee ; how often would I have gathered thy children together, as a hen doth gather her brood under her wings, and ye would not.   Behold your house is left unto you desolate."

Or consider how He speaks of the compassion and pardon and love of God as absolutely without limit and without condition, but also of turning from His light as utter darkness, and refusing His rule as bringing tribulation such as had not been since the world began.   He never balances and compares and modifies and says this is part of the truth and that is the other, but drives it home as the one truth in the connection in which He is speaking and for the situation with which he is dealing.

This does not mean that you can say half a truth one Sunday and the other, as if it were in flat contradiction, the next.   It has to do with what I have called the elemental, the tremendous issues of life, with its right decisions and its wrong, with its noble faiths and base compliances, with its sincerities and its hypocrisies.   The great things of God touch life in these decisive ways, and you are to speak of them in this decisive manner and be concerned to carry them home in the heart, without being greatly troubled about possible misunderstanding, knowing that as God's truth is one and man's experience can come to be one, what to the intellect are seeming opposites should end in a faith which can harmonise them all.   There are diversities of operation but the same Spirit, and He is not less one Spirit for the diversities of operation.   You do not need to go beyond fundamental truth to find diversity, for this alone touches men's lives and hearts with endlessly varied experience.

As you go on in life the earth may

> take a sober colouring from the eye
> That hath kept watch o'er man's mortality.

Yet you should be able to say to the end,

> O woeful day, if I were sullen
> When the earth herself is adorning
> This bright May morning.

And if you grow in genial wisdom and large sympathy and insight, you may keep watch over the faith and hope and love which speak of what abides for ever, as well as over the fleeting life which passes as a tale that is told.

There is law and there is gospel, and there is gospel in law and law in gospel. There are the rocky steeps of Sinai and the green pastures of Galilee, there are parables by the lake and the sword piercing through the soul on the way to Calvary. Always to be denouncing, always to be pleading, always to be in the depths or in the heights, always to be using the moral whip or always to be supposing that nothing is involved except ' my yoke is easy,' is just to miss the one great thing in life that is worth preaching about, all its height and its depth.

To this end we ought to pray : ' Give us freedom, give us quietness, give us expansiveness.' But this is all summed up in ' Give us a heart at leisure from itself,' which can only be assured by the peace which the world cannot give or take away, because we have committed our immortal as well as our mortal welfare into wiser and stronger hands than our own, and are anxious for nothing, not even our own souls.

X

FERVOUR AND ITS SUBSTITUTES

A SUPREMELY great message of urgent practical importance should naturally give the warmth to speech and the elevation to style which we may call fervour. Though this should spring too directly from conviction to be a mood, it should be responsive to all moods that are responses to life's variety.

So effective is genuine fervour for public speech that, when lacking, there is a strong temptation to provide substitutes. The most familiar are unctuousness and turgidity. If these are not moods, they can take possession in the same monotonous way as moods.

True fervour can be won by the method of the Psalmist, to muse on all the works of the Lord till the fire burns, and only thereafter speak with your tongue. Then it will have something of the variety of the lights of nature, under which you may gratefully pass a lifetime; whereas the substitutes are monotonous artifices, coloured lights which may be a good show on occasion, but would be of an intolerable monotony even for a period not very extended.

Unction however is not to be identified straight off with unctuousness, nor rhetoric with turgidity.

To preach with unction was once the highest praise, a sermon without unction being described in homely phrase as 'meat without gravy.' And if it be the juices of the various meats, heightening their own particular flavour, and not an extraneous compound added to it, making all taste alike and none delectable, it is rightly approved. Nor may you wholly disapprove of it, even if it show itself in some measure of intonation,

101

so long as this is unconscious and the natural expression of an overruling feeling of reverence.

Had we a stronger sense that surely God is in this place, we might also naturally fall into solemn and even rhythmic tone.   And if it is like a metre which sustains and exalts thought, a cadence whose measure is loaded with meaning and feeling, it can be to edification.   There are chants which have come down through long centuries of religious utterance which carry fixed associations of worship.   But while this on occasion can have the most moving effect, the imitation of it in monotonous pulpit drone or meaningless rising and falling cadence is like a sleeping draught, an irritant if it fail to be a soporific. Therefore you had better not use any cadence, unless you are sure that the mantle of musical inspiration has fallen on you.

There is also a place, not only for oratory, but for rhetoric ; and it would be certain to appear once again, did we ever come to be in dead earnest about anything.

I once heard a young Frenchman addressing a large audience, composed mostly of men who had been through the war.   His subject was what he called Passivism, meaning not that he would not fight, but that security in the end could only be won by friendship. He looked like Charlie Chaplin and he had the same capacity for making every gesture and every line of his body speak his meaning.   He took the whole width of a large platform and what he said was pure rhetoric, with ' vultures on the battle-field ' and multitudes of other well-worn tropes.   But it was fired with blazing con-viction : and he held the fixed attention and even won the approval of an utterly hostile audience, which no other kind of speaking could possibly have done.

On the other hand, I find no kind of speaking less interesting, or for that matter less impressive, than what I may call plateau French oratory, not even the heavy solemnity of the German.   Though both may be heard nearer home, of what we should like to think the genuine English article, I had better in these days of hyper-sensitive nationalism leave the description to Heine, who had so little love for us in other matters that it gave him the same shock to think that Shakespeare was an Englishman, as a German had when he learned the deplorable fact that Jesus was a Jew.

In the English parliament, he says, men do not forget that the joyful kettledrums and trumpets must mingle with the deafening Turkish music of deadly conflict to make it tolerable. Hence " in the most earnest debates, where the life of thousands and the welfare of whole lands are at stake, it does not occur to anyone to pull a stiff German high official face or to declaim in French pathetic-wise." In consequence the speeches can be read with interest long after, while the dreary solemnity of the German serves the purposes of secrecy even when the speeches are published.

How far even substitutes for true fervour can be produced by taking thought is doubtful, because they spring from emotions of sorts, and emotion only travels freely through its accustomed channels. But calculated speech and actions are never its accustomed channels, and nothing shows more plainly than unctuousness and turgidity the effect of flowing freely in the accustomed channels: for when they find full vocal and bodily expression, they turn not only into heat but into steam, like oil flowing over a hot plate.

For producing genuine fervour bodily exercise may profit nothing, but it is highly effective for its substitutes. The text might only be ' Twelve wells of water and seventy palm trees,' but by pulling a long face, waving the hands like a hired mourner at the place of wailing, speaking in whining falling cadences, and following up much repetition of the text with ' O yes, O yes,' not only the sermon, but the soul of both speaker and hearer could be made simply to drip with what is known in our day as the numinous. Or if it be ' What wilt thou do in the swellings of Jordan ? ' and the preacher assumes a brave fighting posture, and with appropriate voice and gesture, eye in a fine frenzy rolling and rhetoric swelling like Jordan itself, demands what philosophers *et hoc genus omne* would say to this great question, not only will his own soul as well as his sermon be filled with a fervid robustiousness, but unless his hearers are very cold-blooded and critical they will be stirred to the depths of their souls.

Heard occasionally, both might be impressive and though you can imagine what either would be as a constant infliction, as some people like to have all natural flavours drowned in pickles, so many thought it was not preaching at all without one or other admixture. Nor, if it is to escape mere flatness of speech and prosiness of diction, are they without justification, for better an artificial flavour than none at all.

Probably you are not much in danger in these days, either of pure turgidity or pure unctuousness. But there are other things which may be merely clothed upon your preaching which are a fair imitation of them. The danger arises when you have little to say and do not feel even this little very deeply. Then it is not in human nature not to clothe it in language which has more sound than sense, and utter it in a tone which comes very near to unctuousness, if not to a still worse denial of all true feeling, which is sentimentality. Speech has been called a device for concealing thought, but this kind of speaking is a device for concealing the fact that there is no thought to conceal. If you have something worth saying, or at least if you come as near it as honest preparation can attain, and if you have meditated on it in face of human need, till it has touched your own heart, you will clothe it in a style which may not be as simple or as clear or as beautiful as you desire, but will at least be straightforward, and you will utter it at least with sincerity.

In the same way, if your style is simple and clear, your thought will be helped to lucidity and your speech to naturalness. And as you should hear yourself speaking when you write and when you think, unaffected speech will do much to save you from putting sound for meaning and spacious platitude for concrete thinking.

Not only does emotion travel freely only through its accustomed channels, but if strong enough seldom leaves them. A person under intense emotion rarely misses the right pause, the just gesture, the appropriate inflexion or even the fitting word. But when feeling is weak or merely simulated, it does not carry away the obstacles, but makes itself still more feebly diffused by damming up its natural channels. Though the Behaviourist is merely exercising the age-long privilege of the learned to be free to talk nonsense, so long as it is sufficiently technical, when he says that we fear because we tremble and do not tremble because we are afraid, fear will increase as you allow its ordinary physical manifestations scope and diminish as you hold them in check. So judgment delivered with soft voice and open palm would arrest any sense of impending doom in the speaker as well as the hearer; and mercy offered in a stentorian voice with closed fist, would not give much comfort to the heart of either.

This is plainest regarding gesture. Suppose that you are making a final appeal, and instead of collecting your force, physical and mental, to reach forward to the goal, you make a feeble, irrelevant, side-ways gesture, it will dissipate the earnestness, first in yourself and then in your hearers. This is why meaningless, merely rhythmic gesture is not merely unhelpful, but is a positive obstacle to all right feeling and response.

On the other hand, when, as Donne says, " It seemed as though her very body spoke," whatsoever words there are will be mightily reinforced. I once heard Gavazzi speak to a North Country audience, who did not understand a quarter of his very foreign English. Yet the expression of his feelings and even of his ideas, in voice and gesture and facial expression, was so amazing that very few would have admitted that they had not understood and sympathised. And this was because the channel of emotion was so perfect that what the speaker felt was sustained in himself and passed to his audience.

Spurgeon illustrates the difference between the natural and the unnatural with pictures of Paul preaching at Athens on an open platform, fitting gesture and every line of his body emphasising his message, with the Rev. Dr Paul preaching in London shut up in a box, his spectacles drooping from his nose, his hands hanging in dejection and his whole attitude a misery to behold.

Though not as evidently, yet as certainly, the same applies to speech as the accustomed channel of emotion. It depends on instincts which are the result of all our growth in response to our fellow-men, and at its best embodies an insight which has been the growth of ages, besides being dependent on sympathy between the speaker and his audience. This cannot be learned; and even if acting fulfil Shakespeare's high requirements of holding the mirror up to Nature, it still comes short of something which is felt even in very bad speaking when utterly sincere.

Garrick speaks of the actor delivering his fables as if they were truth, and the preacher delivering his truths as if they were fable. If this be true, it is a sorrowful failure on the part of the preacher, yet even so, he would not be saved by imitating even the best ways of the actor. And the reason is simple. The moment speech becomes a conscious art, the product of reflection, it ceases to be the accustomed channel of emotion, not to speak of the danger of making the emotion itself merely simulated and wrought-up.

It is good to have a beautiful vocal performance, if this come to you naturally, but it will not impress unless it has also simple downright sincerity. The fervour of intense conviction like a torrent can even force its way through any channel. The most convincing speaking I ever listened to had every defect of elocution that could be imagined, even to imperfect audibility, but it swept down all opposition by the sheer intensity of the speaker's conviction. It was followed by a perfectly uttered oration, but this passed over the audience like water off a duck's back. One felt about the first speaker that to have corrected even one of his faults would have been to limit his power.

And any honest conviction, even if not very impetuous, can force its way against many obstacles.

Many years ago, I happened to hear Hartington and Chamberlain speak, with a short interval between the meetings, and on the same subject. Chamberlain was the finished speaker in every respect, to whom it was a pleasure to listen. Hartington's was a careless, heavy parliamentary utterance. But Chamberlain seemed to say, this is so fine that you must approve of it ; while Hartington seemed to say, I don't care a hang whether you approve or not, it is the truth : and it was the latter, not the former, who made people feel that they were faced with a vital decision.

The effect works backwards as well as forwards. Genuine fervour will naturally express itself in simple and direct style, fitting gesture and unaffected and moving speech. And while no attention to speech or style will ever give genuine fervour, halting or bombastic utterance, awkward inappropriate gesture merely sawing the air, and a ragged, halting or rolling flood of style will check any feeling or, what may be worse, change it from sincerity into mere simulated passion. But though fitting utterance and gesture are far from being irrelevant or unimportant, it does not follow that they can be corrected from the outside by conscious effort, for the moment they are deliberate, conscious, calculated, they cease to be accustomed channels of emotion.

Even mere emotion cannot be increased except by flowing in its unconscious natural channel, but fervour is distinguished from mere sentimentality or mere heat, by springing from the conviction of the reality and importance of a truth. It is possible to try to think with the heart and feel with the head, with the result that the thinking is fog and the feeling the glitter of snow. Yet all good thinking requires enthusiasm for truth and the highest thinking the intuition of the heart. And it is this highest thinking I mean by fervour.

This cannot be won by any art or man's device, but it can be hindered. Therefore all I have to say concerns the smaller, but still very important question of the ways in which true fervour can be obstructed and suppressed. In considering the working of the process backwards, we shall begin with speaking, because it most of all is thought to be an art by itself which can be cultivated apart either from what is said or how to say it.

XI

SPEAKING

THE true order, both logical and practical, is first to have something worth saying, second to express it in a style fitted to convey its meaning and quality, and finally to utter it in such a way as would carry home its feeling as well as its significance. But I take the illogical order, because it is frequently followed : and my main purpose is to question the prevalent idea that the art of speaking may be an isolated acquirement and the initial qualification with which a public speaker should equip himself, without consideration of the intimate inter-relation of thought and style and utterance.

This does not mean that speaking itself is unimportant. There is a kind of speaking to which you cannot but listen, even if what is said is not of supreme significance, and there is a kind which requires constant effort to follow, even when what is said is of greater consequence.

This fact you should recognise, and you ought not to be above learning any part of your trade from anyone who can help. To build a bridge an engineer must not stop at being an authority on strains, but must condescend also upon fitting keystones or riveting bolts, if his bridge is to serve long to carry traffic freely and securely. So your sermon will be a highway for the general public only if it be clearly, persuasively and effectively spoken. But while this is an important result, it does not necessarily follow that it should be a direct aim.

There may come a time when you have developed faults which need to be corrected. But as the first of all requirements in natural public speech is to forget yourself in your subject and your audience, more harm than good is done by drawing attention, at an early stage at least, even to faults.

This includes even limitations in audibility. You ought of course to learn to speak in any building, as far at least as nature and practice can equip you. But you should begin with small gatherings in small buildings, and grow up naturally and as instinctively as you can to larger. To start with audibility as a deliberate aim is likely to make you a follower of the precentor told of in Brown's *Life of Bunyan*, who was subjected to ecclesiastical discipline for singing " in a gesticulous and altitonant voice," which, in spite of the fact that this may be offered you as a model, is a fitting subject for censure.

Teaching speaking as an art by itself is very apt to be like the specialist who treats a throat as if it were not part of the human frame, responsive not only to the general health of the whole body but even to the spirit which dwells within it, and were simply stuck into a graven image.

Public-speaking is neither my foible nor my forte. Now, however, that we see the effect in easy audibility and unstudied naturalness, of Dr Hulbert's method of working from the spirit outwards and not from the voice inwards, I may be pardoned for thinking that my native defects were increased by the painful consciousness of my voice forced upon me when beginning.

As I was obviously in need of help, the advice of my friends was frequent and free ; and I learned too late that it was uniformly mistaken. I was told to speak up when I should have been told to speak more quietly and get weight and force out of my lungs, instead of applying twice the force necessary, to the ruining of my vocal chords. I was told to keep my lungs full when my fault was in keeping them bang full all the time and not emptying them, with the result of making breathing self-conscious and spasmodic. I was urged to be livelier, whereas I ought to have been told to be more deliberate. But the worst was that it gave me the distressing sense that preaching was a business of impressive exhibition, not a self-forgetting task of persuasion.

Were it not for this last possible effect, which may be even worse with his help, the lesson would seem to be to trust only the professional elocutionist. If you can escape the idea of being expected yourself to do professional elocution, and confine your hope of help to the curing of your faults, you can learn from him. Yet his ministrations should be, like the throat specialist, confined to morbid conditions, and as you are restored to health only when you are able to forget that you have a throat, so it should be with the voice. Two or three matters I may however just mention in the hope that you may be able to follow good advice, though not supported by good example.

1. Always accentuate new matter, and only new matter: and a pronoun having an antecedent is never new matter. To this there are only two exceptions. You do not accentuate the negative even when it is new, and you accentuate an antithesis even when it is not.

2. Words carry unconfused to the end of a long building, not by loudness, but by being separated by a soft breathing. The difficulty is that this is not part of the ordinary English speech. A German says Ich' habe, an Englishman Ichabe; a Frenchman says Avez' vous, with the same weight on each syllable, an Englishman runs them together, accents the first and swallows most of the rest. The elocutionist can teach you the trick without trouble, even to putting soft breathings, and sometimes explosions which are not soft, between syllables. But unfortunately for the naturalness of the effect, the English language is not spoken in syllables, nor even in words, but in clauses. The relations other languages show by grammatical forms English shows by order and grouping; and this

may not be sacrificed, even to audibility, without producing artificiality. The difficulty however is not insuperable, but probably you will overcome it the more easily the less, after you have appreciated the fact, you think about it or try to apply any kind of rule.

3. The hearer must catch words to know their meaning, yet hearing is following meaning, not merely listening to sounds. Wherefore you will not be heard on earth, any more than in heaven, for your loud speaking. So long as people are following, they never know what words they are missing, but when they cannot follow, a voice rapping out syllables like a steam-hammer would not prevent them from thinking that they do not hear.

Two notes in particular the speaker is apt to think specially resonant and effective and the hearer to find specially confusing and distracting.

The first is the note or pitch to which the building echoes. If you have an ear at all, you are almost certain to catch this, respond to it and rejoice as it multiplies your voice like an organ coupler. Yet this is the note which above all others drowns sense in sound, and is therefore most carefully to be avoided. Nor is it difficult. Few buildings echo except on a very narrow range of pitch, and if you avoid it, generally by keeping below it, you will often find that buildings with a bad reputation have a quite helpful resonance.

The second concerns the notes in your own voice which are specially penetrating. There are two in particular. The hard, especially the nasal, and the throaty and forced, especially in initial vowels, which can be produced like consonants only in this way. You will be quite right in thinking they carry as sounds, but you are wrong in thinking they carry as sense. They are trying to the speaker, unpleasant to the hearer, and by reason of the contrast make the rest appear feeble and ineffective. When you think a note specially penetrating, follow the cynical advice about what you think specially clever, and cut it out.

4. With all possible freedom of movement, you should still stand firmly on your feet. Talma, the French actor, used to say, " Look after your feet and your hands will look after themselves." For this there are two reasons. The first is that your body is a resonator to your vocal chords as the piano is to the strings : and you cannot play a piano on rubber legs. The second is that, without a firm and decided poise, you will have awkward, meaningless, mechanical gesture.

To be able to speak with comfort to yourself, so that you need not think of your speaking but only of what you have to say, and with satisfaction to your audience, so that they are not distracted by attending to vocables but can give their whole attention to taking in the meaning of what they hear, is a great accomplishment.

Yet the question still remains of how far this can be acquired by direct effort. Is the elocutionist's finished product really impressive speaking ; and does not his method, of starting with breathing and enunciation or with the voice at all, run counter to the fact that speaking is not a natural channel of emotion the moment it is conscious and calculated ?

No doubt direction of attention to the externals of speaking does not disturb everyone alike. But there are persons who find speaking in public on matters which touch them deeply very distressing, whose only chance of winning through is to forget themselves in their message, and to whom any suggestion of voice production merely gives the painful sense of being expected to be a successful pulpit performer.

If it be true, as Dr Hulbert maintains, that if only Philip's question to the eunuch, " Understandest thou what thou readest ? " is properly rubbed in, breathing, accentuation, inflection, pace, and all the rest come of themselves, there would seem to be no justification for beginning otherwise with anyone. Though I am speaking specially for reserved souls who find only

H

themselves as they forget themselves, the result would seem to approve a like method for all, because it helps to make style direct and thinking simple, as well as speech natural and attractive. Anyhow the aim is surely right; which is to make the voice so entirely the organ of the spirit as to be irresistible. To this all other aims should at least be subordinate.

Speaking seems no longer to interest or to move people as formerly. We hear much of the decay of the pulpit, but is there not a greater decay of the platform ? The preachers may be few anyone would go far to hear, and fewer still whose preaching might become a cherished memory: but where is now the political orator whom no one would think of missing, if anywhere within reach, or whose speech would form the topic of conversation for days afterwards ? Nor does the ordinary speaker seem to get a better hearing on the platform than in the pulpit.

The usual explanation is that the people have changed, or at least that their interests have. But are they so very different, or less concerned either about religion or about politics ?

Something similar has befallen singing. Formerly plain working people delighted in singing songs to one another by the fireside. Now they may go more to concerts, but how far do they enjoy what they hear, or at least does it ever move them as the old simple unaccompanied melodies ?

May not the real reason be, in both cases, that something subtly true and appealing has gone from the voice, from singing through the keyed instrument, with its fixed tones and half-tones, and the idea of a performance ; and from speaking by the rigid rules of voice production and the idea of elocution ?

Perhaps the very mention of the existence of his voice either to a singer or speaker, especially at the beginning of his ways, should be condemned as assault and battery upon the finer responses of spirit to spirit. Even the hints I have given, after you have considered how far they are right, you should dismiss from your minds, unless by chance it should occur to you that you are transgressing them.

We may however close with one other rule, which has the highest sanction, and is not likely to make you self-conscious. Begin by taking the lowest place with quiet conversational speech, and wait till some inspiration comes along and says, 'Friend, go up higher.'

Good preaching has been described as 'animated elevated conversation.' It will not be very effective if it is mere talk, neither animated nor elevated. But begin by being sure that it is conversation. Then let the animation come by interest stirring your imagination and elevation by the impression of the greatness and sublimity of your subject. If you try to impose animation, it will end in our friend the precentor's 'gesticulous and altitonant voice,' and if you think you can raise yourself to elevation, it will only be getting up on stilts, from which you can neither rise higher nor descend lower.

The old ideal is sound, if it come natural to you.

> Begin low, speak slow,
> Rise higher, catch fire,
> W ax warm, sit down in a storm.

You can at least begin low and speak slow, even if you have to leave the rest to be as the spirit moves you. Yet always remember that the limits of the voice that has been granted you determine how low and how slow you may speak. You may only begin as low as can be heard and as slow as will not drag. And notice that this tag does not say, 'Speak faster.' The more intense your speaking becomes, the slower you may go without losing the impression of flow and movement.

Some of the greatest orators have spoken with quite amazing slowness : and it is good advice to speak as slowly as your gifts will allow you. But it may not be slower. If you have a full and pleasant voice with great range of inflection and great variety of appropriate gesture and effective pause, you can afford to speak very slowly ; if you have a thin voice, small range of inflection and small natural gift for bodily expression, to do so would be merely boring. Even then you should not neglect the pause, if it is not mere hesitation or a hint to look out for something especially good, but is from a sense that the truth you utter challenges reflection. Otherwise it will be a case of

> Out it streams, this panting diction
> Carries all things save conviction.

Also there are pauses and pauses, distinguished not only by length but also by quality. For example pauses at a comma and at a full stop are not merely or perhaps at all one short and the other long, but one is of a quality which indicates that your thought is going on, and the other that up to a point it is finished. Few faults are more meaningless than period pauses put in like bars in music at regular intervals. Nor should any pause be an interruption, but itself be part of the progress, like the way Cromwell would look round amid the hottest cavalry charge, to see how the battle was faring as a whole.

One other question you may think it necessary to ask. Supposing any trace of a local accent still clings to you, how far should you set yourself, by deliberate effort, to get rid of it ?

If there are errors which are obvious, you may and perhaps should take this obvious course. Supposing, for example, the aspirate to be migratory, it is worth while to take some pains to follow the advice of Polonius, and ' Neither a borrower nor a lender be.'

Matters of tone and inflection and purity of vowels may still more limit the number who understand and not be pleasing to those who do. But they are more difficult to correct without loss and without artificiality, at least consciously. Half-conscious response to what you hear about you is one thing and deliberate imitation of what you understand has cultural approval is another. There can be really fine and effective speaking which would lose much without the flavour of local accent, and astonishing artificialities as the result of deliberate effort to eradicate it. The change of the East-end accent into the speech of Mayfair by even the best teacher of Phonetics takes as much simple faith to believe as anything else even Mr Bernard Shaw's fertile mind ever required of human credulity.

The worst caricature of human speech I think I ever heard claimed Skeat as its father, and only made more aggressive the native parentage by the attempt at concealment. Possibly what is nasal or slurred or monotonous or sing-song may be thus immediately corrected, yet even this may end in worse ; and beyond it the result may be a studied affectation, which, as a vehicle of thought and feeling, is not to be compared with the least attractive among the large selection our country of many races provides. Even the standardised perfection of the wireless announcer, though necessary for his purpose, does not come home very warmly to the mind and the heart. And all questions of speech concern what irresistibly does.

Accents, like other achievements, differ in attractiveness, but is any accent, even the most approved, so perfect as to have a right to play the part of Aaron's rod, and swallow up all the others ? My own I fear rather plays the part of Joseph's coat, as I have lived among many varieties, if not quite from Land's End, at least to beyond John o' Groats, with probably the original dye still as the ground, though an old Irish beggar once appealed to me with confidence as he ' recognised the owld brogue.'

Though the Irish accent is charming, the Irish people are often more polite than precise ; so it may be necessary to flatter oneself by thinking of the saying that the stronger a person's natural quality, the more likely he is to remain racy of his native soil. A Scotswoman, it has been said, should never be trusted if she can keep her feet among the ' shalls ' and the ' wills,' and the ability to pronounce ' rr ' in approved southern fashion might equally raise suspicion. The Scots sergeant who said, "When I say the second syllable of ' Turren ' then turren," was doubtless a very robust character.

XII

STYLE AND SPEAKING

WITH respect to style also, the first question is how far it may with profit be dealt with by itself apart from matter and utterance.

That nothing much matters in literature except style is far from being a new doctrine, though it may have more advocates in recent than in former times. Nor is the idea that it can be put on like a coat of varnish. This is as old in English literature as the Euphuists; and if Jespersen is right in thinking that speech began from the pleasure of making impressive noises, with little concern about expressing meaning, it is as ancient as the human race.

Like most fallacies, it persists because of the truth in it. Great literature must be 'a gem of purest ray serene,' not paste cut into varied and fanciful facets. Yet, unless it is cut and set in perfect form even the profoundest and most original thinking will not make it immortal. Only the word fitly spoken is 'as apples of gold in baskets of silver.' The gold and silver by themselves are for any workman to fashion to better purpose, and only when its form cannot be improved, is it 'a joy forever.' Preoccupation with form, moreover, has the further justification, that perfection in it has probably never been achieved without a conscious ideal and patient labour to attain it.

Shakespeare, 'warbling his native wood-notes wild,' has come down to us with no less authority than Milton. But the man who spoke of himself as

> Envying this man's style and that man's scope,
> With what I most enjoy contented least,

119

was surely a conscious artist, aware of his gifts, though with the modesty of a great mind, which is never satisfied with its best achievement.   Milton himself was certainly very much aware of the task of making his thoughts 'in harmonious numbers move.'   Tennyson, who describes himself, with anything but accuracy, as the 'careless singer of an idle day,' speaks of Virgil as

> Wielder of the mightiest measure
> Ever moulded by the lips of man.

And Virgil certainly did not do it by unconscious art. Plato speaks rather unkindly of poets, but it may be doubted whether his prose came so near poetry by the mere fact that nature had made him a poet in spite of himself.   If Homer is the collection of popular ballads some German critics think, there would be a very impressive exception.   But their own dreary prose and their obvious ignorance of how anything with more inspiration than an encyclopædia article ever came to be written, is just ground for scepticism about the mere dovetailing of traditional material ever making a great poem, without a great poet to shape it.

Yet the care to give noble thought perfect form does not prove that style can be a proper object of care by itself.   You cannot appropriate a style from some superior craftsman, like Walter Pater, or even manufacture it for yourself according to approved pattern. It is not your clothes, but your skin, depending on the health of the whole body, and upon the proper functioning on which the health of the body depends.   The very first quality of a style is that it is your own, a true expression of yourself, the fitting vehicle of your particular way of thinking and feeling.   Hence taking thought for form effects not a style, but a mannerism or even an affectation ; and, as Schopenhauer says, a style which is not our own is not a face but a mask, which in its monotony is more repulsive than the ugliest face.

The professional stylist would say it is at worst

cosmetics, at best health regulations. But cosmetics
are a poor substitute for a natural complexion, and
regimen is only for the valetudinarian, and, even for his
health, of doubtful dispensation.

In respect of form, as of most things, we can say with
Carlyle, when he had finished *The French Revolution*,
after loss as well as toil, " In fine as brave old Johnson
has said ' Useful diligence will at length prevail.' " But
the question is, what is useful diligence as applied to
style ? With Johnson himself, it went far to justify
Goldsmith's retort, when Johnson scoffed at his idea of
writing for children as itself child's play, that Johnson
would make the little fishes talk like whales.

Is attention to style by itself—concern about words
and phrases and balance of clauses and such like—for
its own sake, likely to prove useful diligence ? The
utterance, the form and the substance of your thought,
are not merely closely connected, but are one, and one
style does not necessarily suit the variety of the matter
or the moods and capacities of even one person.

Unfortunately once more we must divide in our consideration what God has joined : and as the preacher
must be specially conscious that what he prepares is to
be spoken, I begin with the relation between style and
utterance.

Words were invented to be spoken, not to be written.
Wherefore even in writing everyone to some extent
hears himself speak, and the public speaker, hearing it
most, is in more danger of having his style determined
by sound than anyone else, though even the person
whose medium is writing, not speaking, does not always
escape. For example, Lowell says that Mrs Browning
always wrote at the top of her voice. Breathless style
goes with panting diction ; unvarying tallness of style
with plateau utterance ; and a style of resonant, mouth-
filling words and phrases with orotund oratory.

Equally, speaking is responsive to style. But as the
style is of more conscious purpose and less instinctive
than the speaking of it, it will be easier to see the

dangers arising from their close association from the effect of speaking on style than of style as speech.

Ruskin, comparing two passages from his own writings as showing the difference between bad and good styles, notes chiefly, that " no word in the latter passage could be changed without loss of meaning," while in the former passage he had searched for alliterations for their own sakes, and chosen words by their sound and not by their sense, which, he adds, is the first element in a bad style.

As he goes on to speak of the influence of Carlyle's rhythm as well as of his verbal precision, he plainly does not think that prose can sound any way it likes so long as it conveys meaning. But he would, I think, say that only the exactly right word, which conveys the true feeling and the precise idea, will have the perfect melody. And, if this interpret him aright, the poets surely bear him out. All good writing is due choice of words, and all great writers are artists in words. Wordsworth would wait weeks for the right word. If you look at the various editions of *The Ancient Mariner*, you will find Coleridge seeking persistently for the exactly just word, which, when found, has the more perfect melody, though sought as the word to express the meaning in its atmosphere of feeling.

You must not suppose that the only danger of determining style by sound is bombast. No doubt if you have a fine rolling voice there is much more satisfaction in 'multitudinous seas incarnadine' than in 'making the green one red,' but nature may not have provided you with the means for doing it justice ; and moreover the present fashion of the time tends to repress the desire. But different people like to hear their own voices in different ways, and in all ways there may be danger.

I shall begin with what we may call the Spacious Style, what some people would call the grand style, the style you deliver with solemn, resonant, impressive tone. " The sun never sets on the king's dominions " might seem to be spacious enough, but this style would expand it to : " As I have had occasion to remark before, the celestial luminary is never at any time wholly below the horizon of the imperial dominions of our most gracious sovereign." I used to attend the ministrations of a preacher who would address the children somewhat in this way : " My dear young Christian brethren, a youthful mind, devoting its budding faculties to the contemplation and practice of beneficence, is one of the fairest objects of meditation this transitory and imperfect scene we call the world affords."

> Nor highest looks have not the highest mind,
> Nor haughty words most full of highest thoughts,
> But are like bladders blown up with wind,
> Which, being pricked, do vanish into noughts.

There are great thoughts and great occasions which demand great expression, and there are men to whom a somewhat exalted expression is the natural form of their way of thinking. As Spurgeon puts it, if you are Alexander you can ride Bucephalus. For most men however it is a form in which they could not say anything, even when they have it to say, and is seldom their best way of expressing themselves. Yet even for ordinary men great occasions might give at times higher reaches of grandeur, and perhaps it is only our thin-blooded critical age that makes us afraid of it. Elevation and dignity and distinction, both of expression and utterance, are fitting, given due justification.

At the same time there is good reason also, in style as in dress, for our ceasing to make brocade everyday wear. Good plain strong Saxon-English is more becoming as well as more useful for the purpose. For this reason religion in particular, clothed in theological brocade, is increasingly and rightly suspected of not being meant for everyday wear.

Somewhat akin is the Polished Style. Yet it is different in itself, and flows from a different idea of speech. In the eighteenth century it was cultivated with special assiduity, being mostly a copy of Johnson's mannerism without his power. Blair was a notable example in the pulpit. Though it was said that he took so long to dress his sermons that they caught cold, their immense popularity shows how the style caught the public taste.

In its perfection it may be a thing of the past. But there is always the danger of acquiring a smooth, flowing style, which also makes a very little go a long way, and were it not that 'men may come and men may go,' it might 'go on for ever.' As it is for certain people easy to acquire, and as it enables one who has mastered it to speak impressively on next to nothing, it did not die with the eighteenth century.

At that time, however, it reached a high point of excellence. This is how it retold the Parable of the Prodigal Son. I take it from Harwood's translation, dated 1768. It begins with : " A Gentleman of a splendid family and opulent fortune had two sons." But it will suffice if I give the reflection of the young man. " I am determined to go to my dear aged parent, and try to excite his tenderness and compassion for me—I will kneel before him and accost him in these penitent and pathetic terms—Best of parents ! I acknowledge myself an ungrateful creature to heaven and to you ! " It ends with, " Condescend to hire me into your family in the capacity of the meanest slave."

Good work of any kind is well finished, and great writers do not leave their surfaces rough or ragged. But this is not real polish which brings out the colour and grain of the material. It is merely enamel, which makes firwood look like mahogany and mahogany like firwood, and only needs to be laid on and daubed well into the crevices. The result is not conversation, and though it may be elevated, it is certainly not animated.

To-day, however, the greater danger is of being animated at the sacrifice of everything elevated. The modern translation of " I will arise and go to my father " would be more like, " I had better get a move

on and buzz along and pop in on my old dad and say,
'What about a new start, guv'nor?'" And when this
attempt to make things lively goes not only with cheap
slang but with 'the deucedly familiar,' it is time to
think of Cowper's warning:

> He that negotiates between God and man,
> As God's ambassador, the grand concerns
> Of judgment and of mercy, should beware
> Of lightness in his speech.

Yet polished periods are quite as inappropriate to such
insistent and weighty concerns.

The Fine Style, though of somewhat different texture,
is also a combination of style and utterance which can
be achieved by taking thought. It is the preciousness
in words which goes with the delicate utterance which
has been trained on repetition of 'prunes and prisms.'
It concerns itself with words and phrases for their own
sake, and mostly for their mellifluousness. Take this
example from a popular novel: "Ah they were grand
days, those deep, full days, when our coming life, like
an unseen organ, pealed, strange, yearnful music in our
ears, and our young blood cried out like a war-horse for
the battle." If you could deliver this in thrilling yet
dulcet tones, all the patrons of the circulating library
would think you a stylist of the first water. Yet compare
the awkwardness of 'our coming life,' the impossibility
of 'pealed yearnful music,' and the doubtful pedigree
of 'yearnful' and 'cried out,' suggesting an unruly
child demanding sweetmeats not the war-horse neighing
for the battle, with Keats' simple words:

> Life is the rose's hope while yet unblown,

and you will recognise the difference between a style
which is like a person who is fine because she is a lady,
and one who thinks she is a lady because she is very
fine.

All good writing is fine writing in the sense of a choice
of the fitting word. Great writers are not only artists

in words, but are interested even in their history, because the right word has the genius of a people, as well as of the individual, both in its sound and in its significance. But to seek for words by prettinesses is like making razors, not to shave, but to sell.

Finally, there is the Flowery Style. It is taken in this connection because it also is of sound, and not of imagination.

A savage, about to engage in battle, first thinks of paint ; and when a writer or speaker begins, he is apt to think first of adornment. And it is better in youth to be florid than to be arid. Time will probably tone down the colours soon enough. Nor can you ever too much express yourself in living figure. Truth so embodied may shine clearly to all minds, as no mere general statement, even of easier truth, ever could.

What is usually meant by a flowery style, however, is not, the exercise of the imagination, to give to what would otherwise be 'airy nothings' 'a local habitation and a name,' but merely sticking in dried immortelles of 'azure skies' and 'rosy dawns' and 'dewy meads,' not because any reality glows in the eyes of the fancy, but because the words appeal to the ear as at once distinguished and familiar. Even growing on their own roots flowers may be overdone in poetry, and much more in preaching, especially if they are chosen merely for their prettiness. 'Do roses stick like burrs?' Yet it is worse if they are paper roses, which are not even as attractive as genuine burrs.

How often figures are from anything but a lively fancy appears in the frequency with which metaphors are mixed. 'Fancy's child' himself is credited with having perpetrated the line,

> Or to take arms against a sea of troubles.

A friend suggests that this is an error from the old pronunciation of 'sea' as 'say' and is 'assay of troubles.' Then you have a vivid figure of resisting assault with all one's might, and all the difference between routine metaphor and living figure. Anyhow you won't become Shakespeare by imitating his lapses.

We should distinguish in this matter between imagination and fancy. Imagination sees a situation, whether of thought or action, in all its bearings and from the beginning to the end ; fancy sees how other situations bear upon it, are like it, illustrate, enforce it.

If you compare the mixed metaphor, which I fear is a frequent achievement of my fellow countrymen, with the bull which is a peculiar gift of the Irish, you will learn something, not only of the differences between these peoples, but also of the difference between imagination and fancy.

This treasure of mixed metaphor I found in a newspaper of Modern Athens when I was a student in its academic groves. " Lord Elcho is always fishing in troubled waters, but he will not deceive this enlightened public by the flimsy veil of Tory oratory, to which he has nailed the colours of his party."

The writer of this glowing sentence had obviously before the eye of his imagination a political situation with an objectionable opponent in the midst of it, which gave him a kind of logical consistency. But it is equally obvious that the figures in which he embodies it are pure conventional phrases, and never for a moment stood before the eye of his fancy.

Put alongside of this Sir Boyle Roche's famous bull : " The right honourable member has let the cat out of the bag ; I smell a rat ; I see it floating in the air : but the Irish members will be the first to nip it in the bud." Here the figures are seen clearly and vividly, but the situation as a whole merely dances as they flicker on the screen, and for logical connection the author did not care a straw.

Figures of speech—and you may extend this to all forms of expression—only avail to light up a subject when both the whole meaning is clear before the imagination and the form in which it is expressed is living pictures to the fancy.

The quality of style is so entirely distinctiveness that we may only be able to say with Linkum Fidelius that 'Style is style.' Yet if this is true individuality, it is from the steady, deep insight of the imagination lit up by the flashes of fancy, and should be like the picture of the dayspring in Job lifting darkness from the earth to show its form and beauty, as when the seal is lifted from the clay to show the impress upon it.

XIII

STYLE AND MATTER

WE now pass to the other aspect of style, which is its relation to the material to which it gives form.

A distinguished Oxonian, whose name I had better not give because he is now the Head of a College, said : " How is it that we pay so much more attention to style here, and yet the Cambridge man nearly always writes better than the Oxford man ? " The question may be, so far as I know, like the question, ' Why is a herring dead heavier than a herring alive ? ' submitted by Charles II to the Royal Society, to which, after the production of many theories, the scales gave the answer that it is not. Yet, on general principles, the order is not, first have a style and then think of something appropriate to say with it, but first have something worth saying and then make all questions of style the effort to say it clearly, fittingly and worthily.

At the same time there are also dangers which arise from thinking only of the matter and not of the speaking or the form, and of getting it merely off your student minds and not on to the minds of your audience.

The first danger is the Abstract Style.

Frequently it has no better reason than slackness in seeking the right concrete word and being satisfied with the vague general one. But the student is also exposed to it from having acquired most of what he knows from books and lectures which employ learned and often extremely abstract language. Nor is there any escape, if you are to attain a point of view from which you may see at least that truth has a unity the deepest thinking will never fully realise, and a boundless horizon which a lifetime of showing its riches can never exhaust.

But this does not justify you in using words like 'connotation and denotation,' 'subjective and objective,' 'transcendent and immanent,' 'self-conscious and sub-conscious,' 'static and dynamic,' in the pulpit, or preaching on 'Mosaism, Prophetism and Christism,' or praying, as I once heard, that we may be delivered from the temptations 'which arise from various concatenations of circumstances.'

This is merely the kind of helplessness which makes people with an inadequate vocabulary eke it out with bad language. Even in prayer we need not suppose that the Deity, like some purists, thinks the English language after the time of the Elizabethans too degenerate to be worth knowing. Yet it will be no gain to leave the old vividness, simple directness, picturesque conciseness and dignity for modern slang, even if it be erudite.

The trouble, however, goes deeper than mere words. The Elizabethans lived in an age of high hope, stirring adventure, vivid interests; we live in an age of rather colourless reflection. Your training also has taught you to reflect and criticise and analyse, more than to see nature and man and God's truth with the poet's, or even the ordinary man's concrete imaginative insight.

It is our boast that our age is highly distinguished from all other ages, because in it 'the schoolmaster is abroad.' No doubt it is progress, and you could yourselves do ill without him. Nor may you wish that your audience had enjoyed less of his ministrations. But while he is the friend of talent, he is rather the enemy of genius, tending to overlay clear, personal, concrete, vivid insight, with what Whitehead calls 'inert ideas'—the burden of mere extraneous information. You may be very far from having anything to be described as genius, yet the preacher's task is much more akin to genius than to talent, and your task is to learn from your teachers only what stimulates your own thought, stirs your own interest and fires your own imagination : and then to turn it still more into living vision and concrete, picturesque, simple language.

The second danger is the Essay Style. Neither your training nor your cast of mind may expose you to mere abstract or technical expression, but it may to this ; and the best literary training and even a true literary insight may only expose you more. Besides, most students begin to write before they begin to speak in public ; and what they produce is to be read by a person who will have to read it to the end, whether it interest him or not, and who will be more critical of its defects than enthusiastic about its merits, while an audience is free to ignore what neither arrests nor interests.

It was a fine training in the War to speak to men who simply rose and went out the moment you failed to interest them. Convention prevents sermons from being moving in this sense, when they fail to be moving in the other. But the hearers are always free not to pay attention and not to come again. Perhaps an essay will not prevent them coming again, for it may be soothing and allow their thought to wander at ease. But it will not arrest attention. And while it is not your business to speak in a way that requires no effort of thought, it is your business to create the attention necessary for the effort.

The quality of the essay is smoothness and progress from one thought to another by gradual transition. But in a sermon the smoothness may be a lullaby and the gradualness a lack of obvious points which clearly mark progress. A style for preaching is one thing and a style for essay writing is another, a style for preaching being rather the language of the market-place than of the schools.

At the same time, it would be common and meagre and inadequate were it not enriched by reading and defined and ordered by writing. This should not mean, what is only too common, a hybrid of written and spoken styles, which has the faults of both, the dull

smoothness of the former and the looseness and com-
monness of the latter. What it should mean is the
animated variety of conversation, elevated by the
conciseness, dignity, harmony of literature, with its
vocabulary enriched by the poetic, vivid, picturesque
literary word, where this is the only completely right
word.

For most purposes, however, the common word is
the best word. When Luther was translating the
Bible, he collected ballads and songs and anything
which would teach him how ordinary people spoke :
and the result is not only a book the common people
read, but one of the treasures of German literature.

Respect your audience and, if you fail to reach
them, doubt your own mode of presentation, not their
intelligence. They have learned in the school of life,
and not only may it have profounder lessons than any
other school, but even its form of expression may throb
with vitality, while the language of the schools may be
remote, anæmic, cold and colourless.

Though I have spoken of these dangers as arising from
thinking only of what you have to say and forgetting
the form, they do not really come from excess of
thought. Have you fully thought anything through,
while it remains an abstraction ? Have you mused till
the fire burns, if it flow out in an even, cold, colourless
stream ? Matthew Arnold, in his *Essays in Criticism*,
raises the question whether we truly know anything
till we can express it in plain, concrete language ; and
it may be questioned, whether we ever feel anything
till we can express it in language which varies in
intensity, is cold and glowing hot, smooth and abrupt,
slow and rapid.

In religion in particular, the expression of it in
simple, varied, popular human speech, embodied sometimes in homely figure and story, which, though rising
at times to the sublimest poetry and the most im-
passioned appeal, never fails to speak to the common
man in his own language, is not merely something of

value for teaching, but belongs to the nature of religion when rightly known.

Not a conscious change of style made the prophets forsake the excited, numinous, traditional utterance of the Dervish, and speak in the language of the peasant and labourer, and write with the pen of the common man, but a different view of religion as a practical business of the common life. What made their presentation of religion sublime as well as simple was a religion of faith and love and righteousness in the workaday world of ordinary people and familiar things, with the incidence upon them of secular happenings.

Nor does our Lord's way of teaching, in memorable story and simple direct word that come home to men as men and linger in the least educated memory, merely speak of a supreme gift for teaching. It tells also of a religion by which the righteousness of the common day labourer or even of the outcast was to exceed the righteousness of the professed leaders of piety and the learned specialists of theology. The first requirement, therefore, is not to acquire a style which combines simplicity with sublimity, but to have a religion which thus naturally expresses itself.

If therefore the danger which arises from concentration on the matter of your preaching is only because you have not thought clearly enough and felt strongly enough, you may still say that useful diligence is profitably applied only when devoted to the subject first and to the expression of it afterwards, with the diligence mainly directed to saying exactly what you mean, as you see it and feel it, clearly, simply, forcibly, persuasively.

Yet a worse danger may await you than even the worst style, which is having no style at all, except prosing on from one point to another, saying many things, which is the opposite of saying much, in a way not pointedly popular but merely maunderingly colloquial.

The trouble with your calling is that you have often

to speak when you have not found anything faintly resembling a burden of the Lord requiring to be uttered ; and that, even on what you have to say, you have not had time and quiet to muse till the fire burns with any clearness of flame. Then you may fall into what has been described as ' the dreary drip of desultory declamation.'

Yet this desperate state of dissolution seldom comes from the hardest and most distracting work. Much more frequently it is from fussing about many things, without concentration upon anything.

As the trouble is slackness, any diligence, even if devoted to such an otherwise subordinate matter as grammar, might be useful.

Speaking by rules of grammar and logic is, as Ruskin says, like walking with a machine to move your feet forward. Like M. Bourgeois, you can learn that you talk prose more easily than by the elaborate analysis of sentences practised in schools, of which the result could only be the prosiest of prose.

When you are fired by what you have to say, by all means be like the potentate whom Carlyle dubs *Super Grammaticam*, and you may even, like St Paul, not always finish your sentences. But if you find that, just because you are not inspired, you have, like Jeremy Taylor, to confess that you have ' lost the track of the nominative case,' you should set vigorously about recovering it. The business of a sentence is just to say one thing and no more ; and when you find that you are adding, as tags, what should be one right word in the right place, that your participles are unrelated, or your double substantives have singular verbs, it is time to bethink yourselves even of grammar.

De Quincey said of Coleridge that he never finished anything except his sentences. Begin there anyhow. A sentence which bears the burden of one idea, and a paragraph which embodies clearly and compactly and separately one movement of your thought, are essential ways of girding up the loins of your mind for addressing your fellow-mortals on any subject whatsoever, and not least religion.

Boswell asked Dr Johnson how it was that, even in the most trivial conversation he never fell below a finished stateliness of expression: and the answer amounted to this, that he had early resolved never to write or speak except with his loins girt. It is a good resolution, and there may be times when you have little else to sustain you except sticking to it.

XIV

MATTER

THE question of matter, to which we now come, we may profitably approach with a story told me by President Wilson. A negro minister of his acquaintance was praying, in a stentorian voice and with enormous emphasis, " More powah, Lord, more powah." An elder touched him on the sleeve, and said, " Minister, you pray for the wrong ting altogether." " What ! " the minister shouted, " is not powah bery good thing ? " " Powah bery good ting," was the reply, " but you plenty powah. What you should pray for is idees."

Yet diligence cannot be applied usefully even to ideas in isolation, and without considering also their form and utterance. We have seen how the expression of them clearly and simply tests the clearness of thinking ; and it would often help to determine whether a thought is worth thinking to consider if it is worth uttering. How, for example, would the circulation of the halfpenny open envelope be diminished were the contents winnowed by the rigid application of both requirements ? As it is, had its flood broken in on Dante's meditations in his day, as it does without a word of apology on ours in our day, he would have given the inventor of it a long spell in purgatory, had he not assigned him to a worse place. How much also that is nasty would never appear in print, if all authors laid Goethe's question to heart : " Why should we write about what we do not want to talk about ? " Nor would so much mere idiosyncrasy and perverted ingenuity masquerade as convincing truth were it dialogue and not monologue.

Wherefore, as we should not overlook the relation of form and utterance to matter, we should bear in mind also the relation of matter to form and utterance.

With respect to them all, three Scripture precepts are to be borne in mind. The first is, " Let your loins be girded about and your lamps burning " ; the second, " Evil company doth corrupt good manners " ; the third, " Every scribe who hath been made a disciple to the kingdom of heaven is like a man that is an householder who bringeth forth out of his treasure things new and old."

Let us take these points separately and in succession.

1. Though you may think that you have already had more than enough about girding up the loins of your mind, it may still be necessary to add that you cannot do it by mere resolution. You must have something for which to gird them and by which to gird them. The summons may be to the great and unexpected and untried, but you will not be ready to meet it unless you are dealing vigorously with your everyday situation, and, at some continuous task, maintaining your power to concentrate and to control circumstances. As students this means having some special study and keeping a good stiff book going on the subject, to which you can set your minds stoutly after being disturbed by distractions.

Nor can you keep the lamp of truth steadily burning so that it may be light even upon the most difficult, dangerous, untried, unexpected journey you may have to undertake, unless you keep it constantly ready. You cannot supply it once for all even with the oil of grace. Grace is not to enable you to do without aught besides. The conviction that he was laid hold of for a purpose only made the Apostle press on that he also might lay hold on it. The assurance that God works the willing and the doing only gave him the more earnestness in doing his own part. The work of the Spirit is not to save you the trouble of filling your lamp with the oil of thought and knowledge and experience, but, like the oxygen in the air, is what gives it, when supplied, clear burning quality.

The brother who said, "I sit down on Saturday evening, look up a text and then commit myself to the inspiration of the Holy Spirit," is likely to show that he might profitably lay to heart the reply once given him, "The God I worship does nothing to condone my laziness," by verbosely producing dull paraphrase and duller platitude.

Of a book named something like *Addresses to my Curates*, a reader said that, though he had just finished it and had a fairly retentive memory, the only sentence in it he could recall was, "When you sit down on Saturday night to prepare your sermon." Behind that modest effort might be the question of what the preacher had been doing with the rest of the week. In the old days in Scotland, when the visitation of congregations was a serious business, this question was appointed to be asked : "Is Saturday alone your minister's book day, or is he always at his calling ? "

If a man is living a strenuous life, reading, thinking, visiting the sick and the aged and the poor, aware that his people live in the midst of God's calls, thoughtlessly and blindly, impressed by the temptations of success and the discouragements of failure, seeing the follies of youth and the cares of age, and knowing the gracious patience of God's high purpose, through Christ's endless love over all, he may commit himself, even if stress of circumstances have limited his preparation, to the inspiration of the Spirit, and may find something in him burning to be said, which will not fail to edify because it has the throb of life in it, and will not be merely filling up the short half-hour at his disposal. But unless his lamp is full, dependence on the Spirit is merely like striking matches when there is nothing to kindle.

2. The advice already given about solid reading may seem inconsistent with the second point of keeping

good company. Stiff books are not often models of
perspicuous, easy, felicitous, flexible style : and if
you read all kinds of books, converse with all kinds of
people, and are in touch with all kinds of experiences,
you may even find the evil communication which the
Apostle says corrupts good manners.

But the Apostle's own communication in all respects
was extremely mixed, and he himself admits that you
can have no communication with evil, in the sense of
having no dealings with it, only if you do not live in
the world at all. Nor if he had confined his intercourse to godly Christian people and shut his eyes and
his ears to all he thought erroneous and misleading or
even wicked, would he have written much of his letters.

But while he made it his business to be acquainted
with the world around him as it was, and never evaded
either error or vice, he did not commune with them as
with the saints who were in Christ or with Christ
Himself : and while ' Give heed unto reading ' might
include less edifying matter in pagan literature than
he quotes, and certainly includes opinions of which he
disapproves, he would not have taken them to his
heart, as for example the Scriptures.

More than most men, I have had to read books written
in abstract, difficult, dull and sometimes formless style :
and I fear my own has been far from escaping con-
tamination. Also I have kept a good deal of bad
company in matter as well as form. My career as an
Apologist began by reading Tom Paine's *Age of Reason*
at fourteen ; and my business in life has led me to
read many worse books since then : and there may be
ground for dubiety about the result. Yet I hope I
have never taken the style, say of Ritschl, as much to
my heart as Goethe's, or the ideas of the materialists
like the faith of the prophets.

The question is not with what do you make acquaintance, but with what of truly inspired literature and
truly inspired life you company as intimate friends
and ' grapple to your hearts.'

If you observe well this distinction, you may be like the parish minister in my native place. When in his old age he was asked what he was still reading. " Just two books," was the reply, " God's book and the Devil's —the Bible and—" well I had better not say which newspaper. Fill it in for yourselves according as you judge of how far he may have been right about the voice he thought he heard in it. Yet the worst possible yellow press, if it were recognised as the worst and mixed in liberal proportion with the best, would not do you much harm, though, as a man is known by his praise, that is by what he admires, the multitude of its readers is not a favourable sign of our time.

3. The last point about the scribe brings us fully to our next subject. You are to have a treasure from which you can bring forth things new and old, to meet the most unexpected emergency and any kind or number of guests. It must be your own, ready at hand, and provided with more than a stock supply for making creditable sermons.

The first question about the scribe who would instruct into the kingdom of heaven, and particularly by the method of preaching, is in what sense should it all be his own?

May he not, to begin with, usefully have a treasure of sermon-helps on his bookshelves, from which he may draw more easily, more copiously, more continuously, than from the meagre store of old information and new thoughts which he has made his own by his own study and meditation ?

There used to be an American publisher who informed preachers that he was of so benevolent a mind that, for next to nothing, a mere bagatelle of a couple of pounds, he would equip them with an exhaustless Golconda of homiletic riches, and for mining in it, an index as easy in its working and as limitless in its bounty as Aladdin's lamp. You had only to turn up ' Patience ' to find a text and half a dozen sets of divisions to choose from, and illustrations from King

David to David Deans, homely or sublime, portentous or ridiculous. Every year I used to receive a large closely printed stiff cardboard circular, mourning over me that I should be so blind to the day of my merciful visitation as not to make every sacrifice to meet the offer of a self-sacrificing publisher.

I once saw the volume, and it really was a sermonic Bank of England, though whether it was ever on the gold standard is another question. It was of imposing bulk and literally bursting its covers with its treasures. Also I have had the privilege of hearing a product of its inspiration. It began mildly, "As Charles Kingsley has so profoundly remarked." Then we had Shakespeare, Dante and Omar Khayyam, after which it was quite homely to come back to Longfellow and 'Life is real, Life is earnest.' This was followed by a few more quotations, which the good man, without undue claim to originality, might have given as his own. The result was a style which ranged from the stateliness of Milton's prose to the homeliness of Mr Dooley. Yet one of his regular hearers affirmed that it was not a circumstance compared with what the preacher could do when in really good form. Even this apparently minor effort was no mean display, but it was like seeing Eskimo dogs that had been tied all round the sledge, for the subject was not advanced, but merely pulled about. One good idea of the preacher's own, and one good illustration which really came from life and which touched his own life, would have done far more in the way of real conviction.

Conceit is not supposed to be much of a security against a fall, but should such aids come your way and be a temptation in a season of barrenness, you might, without thinking of yourselves more highly than you ought, be delivered by thinking that, if you cannot do better on your own, it is time you should consider some honest job with your hands, and give up the idea that your head would ever earn your living. They will not help you to gird your loins and keep your lamps burning, the very use of them being slackness and borrowing other people's lights ; they will not provide you good company, their variety being the most mixed society ; they will not help you to high thinking, their distracting snippets of ideas not being thinking at all ; they will not fill your own treasure and make you a householder in your own right, but only a kind of receiver of stolen goods.

We may further ask how far homiletic literature of any kind will help towards meeting these requirements. Of this I speak in profound ignorance. Material obtained in condensed form elsewhere, you may be able to water down for yourselves. Yet the diluting in due proportion is a necessary art, for distillations from commentaries and such like, administered neat, may not be suitable drink for any average mortal. And as you never find your own way less for studying well the ways of others, you should probably read a few volumes of the best sermons, to learn how this and all else should be done. The more recent you can select for yourselves. But you might with profit mix a little of Robertson's and Brooks's directness with Newman's subtlety and Caird's rhetoric with Ker's pathos and Spurgeon's robust homely vigour with Church's calm and finished utterance. While you may absorb material by the way, it should be rather to study their methods : and even this should be only to have your own critical judgment stimulated rather than to copy any of them, because no method in the end is right except your own.

With this we may take the whole question of studying, not only books but life, for the direct purpose of providing material for preaching.

If you become interested in your work, you will, as the poet absorbs material for his poetry from all his reading as well as all his experience, be continually absorbing material for your preaching. Yet as a poet who is always thinking of writing poetry is not a poet, but merely a rhymster, a preacher who is always thinking of making sermons is not a preacher, but

merely a pulpiteer. The poet of course must give time
and labour to his poetry and a minister to his preaching,
yet both should be only by-products of experience.

"Charles," Coleridge asked of Lamb, "have you
ever heard me preach?" "My dear Coleridge,"
was the reply, "I never heard you do anything
else." Coleridge might be tolerable, but it is unlikely
you would. And even his was often pretty prosy
preaching.

The Apostle said "Woe is me if I preach not the
gospel." But when he said "This one thing I do"
it was not preaching, but "forgetting the things that
are behind and reaching forward to that which is
before." His preaching came from this strenuous
dealing with life, and drew its material, as well as
its inspiration, from ceaseless dissatisfaction with his
progress.

There is a still further question. Your treasury
is to have things old as well as new, and is certain to
have much more of other people's thinking than of your
own. The question is, How far and in what way may
you help yourself from other people's thought or other
people's experience? With respect to helping yourself
from your reading, in particular, this might come to be
a delicate question of morals.

One of the disadvantages of education is the severe
limit it sets to appropriation. A half-educated person
can regard books as written for the express purpose of
providing him with material for preaching, and can annex
freely, not only with an easy conscience, but with pride
in being so learned as to discover it, while a more
educated person might think this kind of 'conveying'
perilously near Touchstone's use of it as a euphemism
for stealing.

Yet no one could preach long to profit who did not
draw extensively on other people. Perhaps nothing we
ever say is all our own. A wise Greek has said that
not to know what was done in the world before we
were born is always to remain a child. We all build

on other men's thoughts and actions, and like insects on a coral reef, the more we can use what has been done before, the higher our own work is likely to rise.

Sophocles did not crown the Greek drama till he stood on many men's shoulders. Greene is quite right in speaking of Shakespeare as tricked out in other men's feathers, for few people have ever annexed so extensively. But then Shakespeare knew, as Greene did not, how to wear them in so characteristic and transforming a fashion that they were no longer borrowed plumes, but his own native dress. A careful study of the prophets shows how freely they all used the work of their predecessors. Yet each had his own characteristic message to his own age. Even Jesus came in the fulness of the time : and it has been said that what distinguishes the Canon of the New Testament from what followed is the knowledge of its writers of our Lord's Old Testament foundations.

In our day there are notions of literary property which can be discussed in the law courts, yet there are more books than ever made out of other books, which certainly do not display greater originality than formerly in dealing with what is borrowed.

> When 'Omer smote 'is blooming lyre,
> E'd 'eard men sing by land and sea,
> An' what he thought 'e might require
> 'E went and took, the same as me.
>
> ．　　．　　．　　．　　．　　．
>
> They knew 'e stole, 'e knew they knowed,
> They didn't talk nor make a fuss
> But winked at 'Omer down the road,
> And 'e winked back, the same as us.

And when you make as good a use of it as Homer, and do it as openly, you can annex as much as you like and approve yourselves for doing it.

At the same time there is a difference between finding a nugget and appropriating a bar of gold ; and there are some matters in which you should depend entirely on others, and some which should clearly be your own.

Sheridan's sarcasm, " The right honourable gentleman
is indebted to his imagination for his facts and to his
memory for his jokes," at least shows that there is such
a distinction.

An older Irish minister who had been consulted by
a younger on this question, said, " You remember
about the priest's portion in the Old Testament ? "
The young man had forgotten, if he ever remembered.
" Well, he stuck his fork into the pot, and whatever
stuck to it was his." Understood aright, this gives
fairly adequate guidance. Whatever cleaves to your
own individuality and you can transform into nourishment for your own mind and heart, and thereby increase
your own reach and power and characteristic quality,
is rightly yours. This may be almost impossible to
define or reduce to rule, but what girds your loins or
feeds your lamp, or widens your vision, or can be put
into your treasure because it has stimulated your mind
and inspired your heart, and your own thought and
feeling have found for it a place in the whole circle of
your experience, is truly yours. Perhaps the essential
point is that it takes its place as experience fitting into
your own whole experience, and does not remain the
mere alien experiences of other people. In practice, as a
matter of fact, it does not cause much perplexity. However you come by your jewels, you should cut and set
them for yourselves, and the best reading is that which
not only gives you the ideas which enrich your spirits
and help you to enrich the spirits of others, but still
more the inspiration which puts you on the track of
the secret mine. Of such help you need all you can
get from any quarter, if by imagination at least
it become your experience and add to your actual
experience and to your interpretation of all experience.
Yet, as Professor Sorley says of all tradition, we are
free in it as our own inheritance, only as there is in
all use of it something both of the sceptic and the
prophet, to select in it and see beyond it.

But while no preaching is of much value which is not

K

drawn from experience that is your own in some sense, I do not mean by it experiences.

Possibly this question of personal experiences, especially religious experiences, may trouble some of you. You may not only feel that you have nothing very profound to offer, but that the deeper any experiences you have may be, the less you can talk about them. Even with your most intimate friends you are reserved about intimate things of your spirits. You may envy those who rejoice in the pulpit as a sort of confessional box of their souls with the blinds all up, but you know that, if you ever forced yourselves to imitate them, the blinds would come down and you would be very miserable behind them. You may then be led to think that you have mistaken your calling, and probably you will never have so immediate and large a popular effect in it as those who easily wear their hearts upon their sleeves.

My whole generation had something of this reserve, and perhaps I was one of the worst of them. So it may be that I am only speaking for myself and showing myself a relic of a vanished past at that, in saying a word for such people. Indeed I have been given to understand that it is now a counsel of perfection to be able to speak of the inmost thoughts and intents of the heart to anyone, at any time, with the utmost freedom, and that even confessing one's sins in public can be so enjoyable that what, as it has been put, the rest of us take in our stride, is exalted for this purpose into heinous offences.

If this expansiveness come to you naturally, there is nothing more to be said. But be sure that it is not forced on you against nature : for if God made you a reserved person, you ought not to try to make yourself a gushing one. Nor is this what should be understood by preaching from experience ; nor in the end will it have the deepest and most lasting influence.

Jesus certainly spoke to all kinds of people and on all sorts of occasions about religion, and He spoke with the authority of one who dealt with it at first hand,

and He related it to all experience, secular and sacred. But a writer who wishes to prove that it all rested on mystical experiences, can find only two meagre texts to prove it and he has to force their meaning. Though Jesus may have spoken of His call at His baptism, and the story of the temptations must have come from Himself, they were connected with His mission, explaining how He entered on it and how He conceived it, and He gave them in the form of objective story, not as inward experiences.

St Paul was not, I think, naturally a reserved person. Yet even he only speaks of his personal feelings when it is forced on him, and he is not very sure of the wisdom of it then. On the whole, the Bible is concerned with all kinds of events and demands and practical commitments and with what God means in relation to them, with remarkably little about psychological experiences or personal feelings at all. This distinguishes especially the Old Testament from almost all other sacred writings, and yet nothing else so authenticates itself as first-hand application of religion to life.

The very words which express it were themselves deeds and not mere studied reflections. The prophets did not arrive at the faith that there is one God, from Whom are all things and unto Whom are all things, by meditating on the ideas of unity and omnipotence and their reflection in their souls. It became a living, all-transforming faith from learning in face of the disasters of their time and men's wickedness in the midst of it, that God has a purpose no evil can defeat, and that for themselves He was greater than all that could be against them. Throughout they were concerned with common people and secular events and drew their illustrations, not from the priesthood and the religious rites, but from such labours as the farmer's and the potter's, to the end of showing that God was concerned with mercy and not sacrifice just among men's common experiences.

Above all, the Master Himself did not present His

religion as experiences, but as experience which found its objective presentation from all the world of men and things about Him. He drew only two illustrations from the professionally religious—the Pharisee in the Temple and the priest and the Levite on the road to Jericho, not much to their credit—but used abundantly the ordinary events in the lives of ordinary people. This shows not merely His supreme gift of teaching, but the kind of religion He taught and the kind of people for whom it was intended.

For this reason myths may embody much more living religious truth than theologies about the Deity expressed in dogmas about His unity, His omniscience and omnipotence, isolated from the common daily experience. Were the Bible all myth, it would be more religious and more true than such abstractions. Such an isolation is like the old science which thought that the laws of reason could determine what things are, if sufficiently revolved in the inner consciousness. The only result, both in religion and science, is to ignore the realities by which God makes Himself known.

But if religion is thus concerned with God in His relation to the world and man, and with a faith which can face all that is most sorrowful in life and most sinful in man, there is no knowledge or experience that can be irrelevant to it, and its embodiment in ordinary human doings and ordinary human speech is of its essence.

My heart sinks when I see only homiletical literature and little improving books on a minister's shelves. But for the reasons just given, it does not beat very high when I see nothing save religious books of any kind. And it beats with a still slower pulse when I find, in talking with their owner, that he is mainly interested in ideas theological and affairs ecclesiastical, and that literature means nothing, and that in the whole kindly race of men, with the vital thoughts that move so warmly in their hearts, their varied avocations, and the joys and sorrows of their manifold experiences, he has only a parson's interest, and that he has not enough human contact to have so much as a funny story about one of them.

We can wrongly defer even to the highest culture, and be confused between its fashions and eternal truth. But the present vehement insistence that religion should only be a crisis of decision about our dealings with a transcendent God, and that progress in the humanities, so far as religion is concerned, is a mere distraction of the Evil One, and all concern with human affairs a descent from the empyrean into the quagmires and mists of time, seems to be a mere denial both that 'the earth is the Lord's and the fulness thereof,' and that ' reconciliation to the God of Whom are all things ' is just victory over the evil and the evanescent, not by ignoring them but by transforming them. Wherefore if you are to be ministers of reconciliation to edification, you will have to know a great deal about the world and man as well as about God. Nor will you know much about God except you learn of Him where He is actually manifesting Himself. The householder who is the perfect scribe instructed into the kingdom of God, would be one whose treasure even of earthly experience is exhaustless. How you may come as near to this as possible by the use of the talents committed to your charge is then the next question before us ; and I can think of no better way than to take it under the rubric of Bacon's aphorism : " Conversation makes a ready man ; reading makes a full man ; and writing an exact man."

XV

CONVERSATION

WE start from 'Conversation makes a ready man,' because though it may help also to make you full and exact, there is little use being either if you cannot find what you want when you want it. Unless the householder can lay his hand on them, his things new and old are in a lumber-room not a store-house. And he should have it all at command, and not merely the familiar and habitual or what concerns some narrow interest, with the rest dumped down anyhow in the dark and only to be hit upon by accident. Real mental resource has more to do with this readiness than with mere acquirements.

With this goes readiness to keep in as well as to bring out, and to use what never seems to be brought out at all, yet somehow is.

As Bergson says, the way what we do not need for our immediate purpose is not brought out into consciousness is even more wonderful than the way what we need comes in. Consider how helpless the historian would be if, when he was thinking about the Restoration, all the historical facts he had ever learned rushed in on him. And this is the more amazing that his method and judgment, on the particular question consciously before his mind, are still making use of all his studies. Or the pianist, for example, may have nothing consciously before his mind except the musical meaning of the piece he is playing. Yet he is using no end of acquired skill and already determined ideas in the performance. Concentration is largely keeping out the irrelevant, but the relevant is a great deal more than what is brought into conscious thought. Nothing we ever really experienced or truly learned is merely stored in our minds, to be forgotten and only recollected when needed. It becomes part of the mind, changing it and being changed by it; and even when we do not recollect it, may still be active in helping us to deal with new situations. The greatest readiness is just having the whole mind at hand.

A poet is said to be one who remembers his youth. We all do, but we cannot bring it out with its living experience still in it or live ourselves back into it. Nor is this limited to the experience of youth. A genius is not a person who has more knowledge and experience than we have, but one who can bring them out new and fresh, not old and musty.

Conversation makes you ready by not allowing you to wait and ponder, by stirring a wider interest, determined by other persons' interests as well as your own, and by the lively challenge of other people's expectations. It is not merely that you may not simply prose on, in the hope that something will turn up, as you may in monologue if you are dense enough to enjoy being a bore, or sit staring at your paper, as you may in writing, if you are still hopeful of wrestling with the powers of darkness, for in conversation, 'as iron sharpeneth iron, so a man sharpeneth the countenance of his friend.'

It has been said that conversation, in Bacon's sense of finished, felicitous interchange on great subjects, is a vanished art. It is even hinted that the College Combination Room has fallen from its high estate of flashing wit, finished aphorism and classic style in handling subjects of large and universal interest, to donnish witticisms and small talk.

Yet even in a College Combination Room a person usually gets the conversation he deserves; and there are still in it a few whose presence guarantees that the conversation will be lively, interesting, thoughtful and often original and on subjects worth discussing. It takes at least two people to make trivial conversation, and you may be one of them. Persons, with the gift for it, can make even the dullest people talk with a thoughtfulness and an interest which otherwise they cannot discover in themselves. If you find your fellow-mortals consistently dull and their conversation consumedly dreary, it is possible that you are merely seeing in them your own reflected image.

Just here the trouble arises. To be made ready by conversation, you must first be ready enough to start it and keep it up to the mark of mutual interest. And of all men the student is perhaps least apt to be a ready man at drawing out other people. His interests are not theirs, and he does not express himself in their language. But if you cannot clear this barrier to intercourse, you will miss much of what is most valuable in your education.

This is obvious when it concerns the learned and wise and worthy. Possibly you may not find them the easiest to get on with. There are learned persons of such extensive, precise information, that talking with them is like conversation with an encyclopædia ; there are strong persons of such decided opinions that you feel with them like a potsherd amid iron vessels ; there are exalted persons who live in such a rarefied atmosphere that you can hardly breathe in their presence. None the less you ought not to miss any opportunity offered of sharpening the soft iron of your minds on their harder steel. And if you are not afraid to show your ignorance or of passing out of your depth, and do not attempt to divert the conversation to subjects on which you can make a display, but respond cheerfully with such questions as you can modestly propound even if they are not very wise, you will almost certainly find them more gentle with your limitations than you fear and more interesting as well as instructive than you anticipate.

Yet you may find more enlightenment as well as interest if you know how to show those who would not dream of having any superiority to you that you claim none over them. Specially this applies to those younger than yourselves.

One of the most remarkable conversationalists I ever knew was an old man who was kept young by being ever ready to sit at the feet of the humblest student, to learn what the new age was thinking. Even when it is a subject of which you are sublimely ignorant, such as whether the Higher Mathematics displays ultimate reality or is as much use for it as an old woman's spectacles, though you may possibly find more light on what you do know than you expect, you will learn at least that there are some things you do not know, which is very valuable knowledge, for, as has been well said, the deepest ignorance is thinking erroneously that you know.

But what most needs the ready man, and makes him, is to be able to converse with people quite unlike oneself, and perfection would be to be able to do it with anyone, at any time, under any circumstances, and possibly on any subject that interests the other person. And it is worth trying, because there is no one you will not find interesting, if you know how to interest him ; and few whose conversation will not be to profit, if yours is profitable to them. Nor should you draw the line at the strictly moral or even the strictly sober.

If a person made genial by the doubtful means of stimulants, wishes to talk to you and you draw in your skirts and say " You are not in a fit state to discuss serious subjects," you may get the reply given before, " I am not drunk, I know that, but I can't be as sober as I thought, or I would not be talking to so impolite a gentleman."

One day while changing at a junction, I passed a big country-looking man walking after a little wife, with some of the modern confusion about the axiom that a straight line is the shortest distance between two points ; and I did not think that what he had taken on board was too much Higher Mathematics. I was scarcely seated in my corner when I saw him in the other corner, standing up and holding out his hand.

" Put it there," he said. " You're a parson are you

not ? " As I was in mufti, I said, taking his hand,
" How do you know ? " " You're a learned sort of
cove. It's written all over you." To an impeachment
so flattering to my calling I had no difficulty in pleading
guilty.

Sitting down he went on. " Parson's a good sort,
usually a real good sort. The working man thinks it's
conceit when he doesn't speak to him. It's nothing of
the kind. Parson's not really conceited at all. He
doesn't know what to say, and he doesn't know how
it would be taken if he did. What I say is, Don't
let us have any jealousy. Let us all be good friends
together. I admit I have been having rather too many
friends seeing me off this morning, and my wife, who
is first-rate at her own job, but is an ignorant sort of
woman on high principles, thinks I am not fit to be
talking to a learned sort of bloke like you. But I've
brought up ten of a family, and why should I not speak
to anybody ? " I said that, if he had brought them
up respectably, he was fit to speak to the king. " There
now," he said, turning to his wife, " I told you he
was a good sort and as full of sense as an egg's full of
meat. Now what I say again is, No jealousy, but let us
all be real good friends."

This last remark is the heart of the matter, but the
hint about the misunderstanding of the parson, through
his helplessness in opening up a conversation and his
lack of readiness in finding something fitting to say, I
pass on for your consideration.

This acquaintance had only gone a little far in
geniality on probably a rare and special occasion. But
I once received a still more needed lesson from a man I
mainly knew in connection with heavy bouts of drinking.
One morning he turned up, obviously after one of them.

" I never forgot a sermon," he began, " that you
preached on building a wall to the battlement of your
house." " Yes," I said, " that was one of the few
temperance sermons I ever preached." " It was," he
said, " and the best I ever heard." " You have not

been practising it, I see." "Not lately." "Was it bad this time ? " " Very." " Would a shilling be enough to start you again ? " " More I think might not be wise." Strange as it may appear to you, I did not think that sermon had wholly missed its mark, because I saw the wistful earnestness of one often defeated, but not yet despairing of the warfare. Anyhow, it was a great lesson in what we often forget :

> What's done we partly may compute,
> But know not what's resisted.

To realise this ignorance is the first requirement of the charity which hopeth all things and believeth all things.

An American preacher said that he was no good at preaching to anyone except boys and bums. I had to ask what ' bums ' are, and was told that it was American for publicans and sinners. Though I fear I should be a poor hand at either, if I were to write a book on ' People I have known,' the chapter on Bums would be much the most interesting.

Among other valuable lessons not included in any recognised curriculum, I have learned from them that there may be very genuine religion with queer notions of it, very sound and strong character with primitive standards about property, and a real gift for presenting reality and even truth with antique disregard to literary conventions.

In the labour colony at Abancour in the War I met a lad who had been brought up in the most religious kind of Congregationalist home, and had never before met anything but the most reputable people. " I have been learning a lot about men," he said. " There are between thirty and forty of us in our hut, and there are five of them who talk as freely about the prisons they have been in as other men of the places they have visited on their holidays.

" ' Have you been in Pentonville ? ' ' Twice.' ' What for ? ' ' Burglary once ; mere pocket-picking the other time.' ' Was the beak right ? ' ' Oh, the fairest old buffer.' 'Treat you well?' 'As well as could be expected in the circumstances.'

"And the curious thing," my friend added, "is that if you take care to have your kit locked, you could not find kinder, friendlier people anywhere, or any more ready to give you a helping hand if you need it." It was the old story about the publicans and sinners.

The more people differ from you probably the more they have to teach you. And this applies to conduct and, at least in the formal sense, even to character, as well as to station, education and personal idiosyncrasies.

But though it is very necessary for your calling to have touch with all kinds, it is even more necessary to have readiness in talking with plain good people.

If you do not learn something of the large contentment, which is better than all possessions, from people who, though they have no possible outlook upon any of the joys and blessings and activities of this life, not only have the hope of a better world, but never lose interest in the world about them or sympathy with the young and active and hopeful, it is that you are a poor scholar, and not that you have not a good school.

For all this the first readiness is to be yourself and accept people as they are and, in quiet response, to lay your minds alongside of theirs. No one will ever interest you in conversation if you do not know how to interest them, and you cannot unless you are interested in them.

Conversation both requires and makes a ready man. Yet, important as it is, this is not all. It may also help to make you full men. As you draw most of your knowledge from books, you may not realise how many are indebted to conversation for all they know and how well it serves them. Nor perhaps do you even know how great your own debt is.

Even in ordinary learning, oral instruction does what books cannot do, and is best when it is actual conversation, the pupil as free to speak as the teacher, and anyhow by the contact of mind with mind.

At one time it was almost the sole method of instruction, and there is much more to be said for it than the bookworm realises. The great teachers, like Socrates, preferred to draw truth out of their pupil's own mind rather than to give them merely instruction. The supreme teacher in conversation was Jesus : and frequently by the same method of drawing it out by questions like, " How readest thou ? " And when He was asked questions, His answer was sometimes to show that it was the wrong question, and that if you ask the right one, you are yourself able to give the right answer. You have only to change your question from, Who is my neighbour ? into Unto whom am I neighbour ? to have no perplexity about your relation to anyone.

Even to-day there are people remarkably well educated mainly by conversation, and especially among the skilled workers.

Life has brought me into very close contact with men who earn their living with their hands, and I have discussed many questions with them greatly to my profit. In the War they raised such questions as, What is God doing in this business ? Are fatalities providence, fate or merely blind accident ? What is the use of talking of conscience, when the Germans are fighting us as conscientiously as we are fighting them ? Their strong sense of what was right and just, their earnestness, fairness and courtesy in debate, their power of expressing themselves in simple, forcible, and even felicitous English, and the certainty that someone would say the right thing in the right way, would have been difficult to find in a better form in any company. If their knowledge was more limited than a scholar's, it was closer to life and readier to hand than most scholars manage to keep theirs. The university and college are great opportunities if you use them aright, but they are mere blinkers if they do not make you more humble to learn the real life of man and the actual ways of the world.

We may go further and say that there is no acquirement

which will be ready to your hand, unless it is in a sense by conversation. Merely swallowing books is of little profit. Right reading is putting your own mind, sympathetically and expectantly, yet critically, alongside of the author's mind, asking how far his thinking is wiser and juster and better instructed than yours and how far your whole view should be modified by his, or if not, to give reasons for your disagreement. And with all life's experiences it is the same. If they have meaning and value for you, it is because they have enlarged your own experience and expanded your whole view of life as it were by mutual intercourse. Thus only does it become the treasure of one householder—one meaning, one experience; and then and then only you will find what you want when you want it.

Of much debate the usual, almost the uniform result is, 'A man convinced against his will is of the same opinion still.' Even the best logic cannot prove truth. It only arranges our thought about a proposition so that we cannot help seeing that it is true or false. Profitable discussion is possible only when all the parties are in earnest about the truth and the truth alone, and are considering each other's views in order to advance or to correct their own. Then even the utmost difference of opinion may forward understanding, and it is always a gain to see clearly why you differ; whereas a mere debater can make the most trivial disagreement an antagonism.

But conversation may also help to make you exact men.

Nothing demands so much from a writer as dialogue. It must be concise, felicitous, apt to the situation, varied, unforced, lively yet without studied cleverness. Shakespeare's dialogue, for example, is so exact to the characters and the situation that even his greatest utterances suffer loss in mere quotation. If Scott could have written English as he wrote Scottish dialogue, he would have been a very great writer indeed; and there is nothing so precise and felicitous in Hardy as his dialogues of plain folk in dialect. Moreover both probably heard most of what they wrote and did not invent it. Face to face with actual situations and the challenge of immediate exchange of idea, many people have an accuracy of thought and a precision of expression which utterly fail them without this stimulus. They simply prose on in monologue and sprawl diffusely on paper.

I have dwelt on this matter somewhat at length, first, because it is of the utmost importance for your whole ministry that you should know your fellows in this way ; and second, because your preaching should itself be conversation. The hearer as well as the speaker should show his mind, even if only one be vocal ; with all possible preparation, there should be also readiness of response, almost one might say of repartee ; and there should be the touch of mind with mind which makes words go farther than their mere dictionary meaning. It is this specially which would make the common people hear you gladly and with true understanding : and if you do not hear them gladly, it is unlikely that they ever will hear you gladly. Moreover, only by yourself learning from conversation will you ever realise the power of speech really spoken over the printed page, and win faith in the incalculable effect that may come from hearing, and therefore from preaching which truly makes men hear.

XVI

READING

I<small>F</small>, during what we hope will be a long lifetime of service, you are to continue to bring forth things new and old, your treasure cannot be too well supplied. Wherefore it would be a sufficient reason for observing diligently the injunction to 'give heed unto reading,' did reading do no more than Bacon claims for it, that it makes a full man.

Yet as information is little use unless it enlarge your own experience, and the thoughts of others unless they are a challenge to your own, there may be more profitable uses in reading than even filling your minds.

Reading too should be conversation and make you ready; and if you read mainly what is compactly thought and concisely expressed, it should also help to make you exact: and there are no better tests of the books you ought to read than that they challenge your thought and have this quality of exactness.

'Challenging,' however, does not mean dogmatic, nor 'exact' definite and final. Man's knowledge, in almost all departments, ends where we most want to know: and the reaching out to what is beyond is the supreme endowment of the human mind. The highest aspirations of the heart, the deepest thoughts of the mind, as well as the fullest meaning of the world and life, are all in chiaroscuro. Wherefore we must not only be asking for what we know we want and seeking for what we expect to find, but as life is to serve a higher purpose than we know, we must be continually knocking at the door of what is beyond our guessing. The most inspiring books are just those which so far set it ajar as to increase the sense of mystery, not as Ritschl said, as

160

merely another name for what we do not know, but as
something felt like the infinite depth of the sky, which
has the same significance for our common ways as the sky
for the earth beneath it. This is a finer exactness than
mere definiteness, something which says, if expressed in
Scripture language, both that God is found of those who
seek Him and that no one by searching can find out
God. What can be so known it presents concretely, and
the translucent depth of the infinite beyond is still a
definite feeling and not abstractions and vague talk of
the immensities, which is not light and penumbra, but
merely fog breaking up the light itself into worse than
darkness.

Clear light at the centre, shading into deepening
mystery, is the quality of all true literature. There is the
the Greek with daylight clearness in presenting human
life, and the mystery of fate over it. There are Dante
and Milton, who with all their definite theologies and
cosmologies, never forget that, for the greatest, the
spiritual eye is ' dark, dark, immeasurably dark, total
eclipse.' No one ever presented life with such felicity
and fulness as Shakespeare, but the mystery which
surrounds our little moment of conscious time over-
shadowed him almost as an obsession. *Faust* makes
plain that even Goethe, though more a child of this
world than any of them, found his deepest thoughts
before this door of the unknown. All are marked by
insight into life deepened by the sense of mystery, and
the sense of mystery by insight into life.

Wordsworth thus expresses both :—

> While with an eye made quiet by the power
> Of harmony, and the deep power of joy,
> We see into the life of things.

And

> that blessed mood,
> In which the burthen of the mystery,
> In which the heavy and the weary weight
> Of all this unintelligible world,
> Is lightened.

L.

It is lightened because the power of harmony, which the poet supremely possesses, gives the assurance that what is unintelligible to us is the harmony of a greater mind than ours.

The Bible also has this double interest in man's life and the life of things, seeing them clearly and practically in their everyday insistency and also as reflecting eternal realities, now only partly and darkly yet giving the hope of knowing as we are known.

Job, Carlyle once spoke of as the greatest of all that is called literature; and by this test nothing is greater. The lesson of the book is not that man is so ignorant and God so much above his knowledge that he should accept by 'the hearing of the ear' the proper doctrine about God's righteous rule, and that criticism is blasphemy. On the contrary, it is that, when we look at life with deep insight and penetrating imagination, and see its agonies and confront its problems, we know of our own knowledge that we do not understand because it is too wonderful for us. Only when, in answer to God's command, "Gird up thy loins like a man, for I will demand of thee, and declare thou unto me," Job takes courage himself to demand and ask God to declare, does he learn that what even God cannot yet declare to him is light inaccessible, and not darkness.

Ecclesiastes, with its vivid insight into the vanity and mystery of life, is in the canon; Tobit with its cocksureness is not. In all the prophets, while there is an assured conviction that God is continually saying, "Come and let us reason together with human reason and conscience," there is always the reverent sense that He is God and not man. Matthew Arnold contrasts the way in which God is spoken of, as if He were just a big man in the next street, with the prophet's view of Him, as a 'power not ourselves that makes for righteousness.' And, while God, for the prophets, is not—to use the modern catchword—a mere 'Other' in that sense, but One Who is a person and deals with us as persons, One Who says "Stand on thy feet and I will speak with thee," as one person unto another, His thoughts are above our thoughts as the heavens are above the earth.

Still they are thoughts for our thinking and ways for our treading: both to be learned by living in accord with them. The supreme significance of the Bible is that it was lived. Every word of it is as it were an act, facing life in all its joys and sorrows, all its aspirations and degradations, all its loyalty and self-regard, all its justice and unrighteousness and especially all its calamities, and thereby pressing nearer the great mystery of a God Who hides Himself, yet is hidden only in a purpose beyond man's heart to conceive, which though knowledge too wonderful for us, is still in the line of our highest hopes and aspirations.

If you are reading the Bible aright you will always be making discoveries, and you do it most, as with other books, by reading it in the original. But if you consider the beauties as well as the profundities of wisdom Ruskin for example finds in the Authorised Version, you will learn from what you have missed how much more insight than erudition means for reading. And you may often be humbled to learn with how much more exactness and insight plain people have read the English version than you have with all your learned apparatus. There are people remarkably well educated and with a most felicitous command of English, whose reading went little beyond the Authorised Version. Other translations may be useful as commentaries, but we have yet to find its rival in reproducing the simplicities and sublimities of the sacred writers.

Yet while you cannot know it too exhaustively, it is possible to know it too exclusively.

Hazlitt quotes the saying, 'I fear the man of one book': and adds, "So do I, he is usually a bore." And this can be true even of the Bible, though it is not a book, but a library. Read with a fine, penetrating, appreciative spirit which has wide and deep experience of life, it can be a liberal education. But the more usual effect of reading it without other reading is quotations often ill-understood, or doctrines the original writers never formulated, or prophecies of which they never dreamt, or theories which were never before them. Of all the bores I ever met, one who quoted the Bible like a concordance for every crazy fancy was the worst. And a most sensible person in every other respect, who seemed to think that not only the Bible but all literature was written for the sole purpose of proving Seventh-day Adventism, was little better.

This may warn you that width of reading is little use without breadth of mind. But to read literature of any kind is just to read for breadth of mind. And if it is literature, and not merely printed matter, it can hardly fail to help. Unfortunately the bulk of the reading to-day is of printed matter which the reader does not even propose to remember and much less to ponder. Mostly this replaces all serious reading, the Bible with the rest, by what has shunning seriousness as its unique purpose. Yet the masses of stuff written about great books—learned, edifying, and the rest—which have seriousness as the sole distinction, may also snow them under by creating the impression of their dullness and futility.

But while great books themselves and not books about them should be your staple diet, perhaps no one has ever been a great speaker who was not an omnivorous reader. You may even reach a state of mental lassitude at times, when an equivalent of pushpin, like detective stories, may be as good as poetry. If I have to give an account of every idle word I have read as well as spoken, I shall have a long account against me : and if I am growing less tolerant and reject much that, for the moment at least, holds the stage, as sloppy sentiment in diffuse and deplorable English, or pretty nothings dressed up in recherché words and elaborate metres, it may be less improvement in taste than inability any longer to move with the times.

If one lives into a new age, the fact of having lived

in another is no excuse for not trying to understand the world which still harbours him. But a veteran cannot help carrying over some standards from the past; and what seems most perplexing about much recent writing, especially poetry, is the difficulty of discovering any standard either old or new. This is the more perplexing that there seem to be standards which belong, not to the Victorian era alone, but to all literature in all the ages, the observance of which, with supreme effectiveness, seems to be just what gives abiding value to the classical works of the Ancients as well as the Moderns.

An American writer has declared that it is folly to waste labour on the writers of earlier times, as their work has all been creamed by the Moderns. Many books are made up out of others; and America has contributed her full share. Unfortunately the result is not always cream, but has a nasty trick of turning out to be skim-milk.

Encyclopædias of course cream information, and the logical outcome would be to read nothing else. Erroneous as the saying is that the true university is a library, even it would be necessary only for those who write encyclopædias: and while they betook themselves to the British Museum, the rest would feed their souls by reading through the *Britannica*. Especially in the education of theological students, were all the proposals for the extension of their studies accepted, no other text-book would be necessary, or without many more years than is given to the curriculum, possible.

If being a full man means being crammed with up-to-date information, Bacon, having been badly supplied in his time with such aids to want of reflection, was rather empty, and having unfortunately lived so long before this enlightened age, was deplorably in arrear. But try to write an essay in his style, and see if you can bring forth from your treasure as much wisdom new and old. Plato was still more an ignoramus, measured by modern knowledge, but try to copy his grasp, his insight, his style. You might as well argue that it is a waste of time going to the National Gallery because you have prints of its pictures in your study, or that you should not be interested in seeing the original head of Jupiter, because there was a copy of it in plaster, with an even greater air of antiquity, which you looked upon every day in your Greek classroom. You only begin to know what art means when you see the difference. And you only begin to know what literature means when you recognise the stamp of genius which cannot grow old and cannot be imitated.

Possibly too much time was spent in the past on classical scholarship. Yet my only regret is that the time I spent was not better directed, for the little I did plough through gave me my first idea of literature, increased my power to enjoy it, if not to write it, and gave the bleak but very important knowledge that most of our thoughts had been thought not only before us but before our age, and that there were great men before our modern Agamemnons.

All kinds of defects in our present system of theological education are vociferously insisted on, but I am not sure of ever having heard what seems to me the chief defect even mentioned. This I take to be ignorance of literature, and more particularly English literature. In preaching, this seems, often at least, to be the reason why there is so much argufying and rambling remarks, without order, form or distinction. It is not that preaching should be a meticulous literary product. Probably no great work, even of literature, ever has been. But if it flow easily, naturally, spontaneously into its channel, it is because the channel had already been dug by a mastery of fine and felicitous form, which is the more individual from making use of the work of all ages.

Inspiration comes largely from keeping company with the inspired ; and for such inspiration as you have, the expression of it with simplicity, aptness and flexibility, will come better by the unconscious influence of example, than by conscious effort after a style.

An even stronger reason for thinking that the

greatest addition to our present system of theological
education, perhaps of education generally, would be
more familiarity with literature, and more immediately
our own, is that literature is a direct and immediate
expression of the actual movements of a people; whereas
philosophy and theology are only later reflection on them,
often when they are already passing. Wherefore a specialist in philosophy or theology who is not somewhat of
a scholar in literature and history, is as unprofitable as a
specialist in literature or history who is not somewhat
of a philosopher and theologian.

Though at best only a general reader either in literature or history for my own delectation and profit, and
without much knowledge of what more erudite persons
think of it or perhaps much interest in knowing, I make
no apology for speaking of it, because this is precisely
the kind of reading we are considering. Nor may the
fact that the reading is not up-to-date be a very grave
objection, for while the literature of your own time is
the voice of your time, you cannot tell its quality except
by a standard derived from the old, nor even know
whether it is new or, as has often been the case, the forgotten fashion of yester-year, and not even the antique.

But if you must reflect for your own time, as well
as in it, why disturb the enjoyment and profit of the
literature of the present, with the limitations of my
Victorian ideas in particular? You know of course,
from the cinema and similar authentic sources, that it
was a very stuffy time : so if I think we had a little
advantage over the present age in what we deemed no
small distinction, in the days when Carlyle, Tennyson,
Ruskin, George Eliot, Matthew Arnold, Freeman,
Froude and quite a few people besides whom we thought
no small beer, were still alive, and Browning and Lowell
had actually spoken to us, and we knew people who had
seen Scott and many who had heard Dickens read his
own writings and an intimate friend of Thackeray's
walked our streets, you can say here is a relic of that
notoriously self-satisfied age. And we did have in this

literature great satisfaction, and made it the central subject of all our discussions. Living writers roused most conflict, because we took Shakespeare and Milton and at least some of Wordsworth as gospel, and the cult of Chaucer and Spenser and Shelley and Keats was of the inner sanctuary to devotees, where we worshipped and did not wrangle. Even if this seem outworn, you will excuse a native for having an exalted view of his spiritual fatherland, and perhaps add a little from this survival to your study of us as past history.

But the real reason for special interest in the nineteenth century is that every age looks down on its immediate predecessor and reacts from it. This is perhaps a necessity of progress, but it is a great cause also of lack of breadth, balance and continuity. If the twentieth century is not enthusiastically appreciative of the nineteenth, the nineteenth could have no cause of complaint, for even the worst that is said of it at present is mild compared with its high sniffing superiority to the eighteenth. And the eighteenth could not justly complain of it, in view of its own judgment of the seventeenth. That the seventeenth set no great store by Milton, its only supreme poet, and thought the rest of its literature superior to the sixteenth shows to what absurdities this temper may lead. But the nineteenth lost much strength and indulged in much emotional exaggeration from mere reaction from the eighteenth: and as it may be that the twentieth suffers from a similar reaction from the nineteenth. To learn to be fair to the immediate past may be of the first importance for a right use of the present.

XVII

LITERATURE AND HISTORY

Oɴ the subject of poetry in particular my limitations may be most evident. But if much recent poetry seems to me marked mainly by extremes—in substance, more soft than gentle, or more violent than strong, and in form, not very melodious prose in not very graphic terms or metres too elaborate to soar and words too recherché for the menial office of serving thought—you can say that, though I have lived into the present age, it has not been with sufficient freshness to appreciate its merits. Or you may take a kindlier view and think it a case of 'no one having tasted old wine straightway desireth new, for he says, the old is good.'

Yet how are you to know that the new is better if you do not know the taste of the old, and should not both be tested by the standards which have been approved in all ages? Wherefore it may be worth while to ask at least what the qualities of great poetry may be. The limitations both of this age and the last may deny us a very adequate answer, but we may succeed a little better by joining forces.

It is possible and may be profitable to read the poets for other reasons than their poetry. You may legitimately enjoy Pope's biting wit, epigrammatic conciseness and clever brilliance, without feeling any of it to be very poetical. Dryden's more genial and clever lines on the poet laureate of his time as the chosen of Dullness:

> The rest to some faint meaning make pretence,
> But Shadwell never deviates into sense,

is so felicitous as perhaps to be poetry, but it will not be for its poetry that you remember it. Many people read Shakespeare for his psychology, his wisdom, his sheer ability, his quotable sayings, even his knowledge of law or hunting, and Milton for his religion, his moral fervour, his eloquence, without much concern about their poetry. Books have been written on Browning's views, with much interest in what is least poetical in his work, because these uninspired utterances say what the authors themselves think, in a way not too imaginative for their comprehension. Masefield's *Dauber* appeals to me as poetry, but still more because it speaks to my knowledge of the sea and my love for struggling humanity. *The Testament of Beauty* is pleasant and profitable reading, but Plato would have been more likely to enrol the author as a philosopher for his reflection than expel him from his Republic for alluring metres and unbridled fancy, more particularly as Plato himself, both for melody and myth, was much the greater sinner.

Though these are good reasons if no better is forthcoming, a poet stands or falls by his poetry. This means first of all that his thoughts 'in harmonious numbers move.' Though not confined to metrical form, metrical form is part of this, and the test of it is that it makes the thoughts move harmoniously. As this is often felt merely by familiarity, it is easy to condemn new metres too hastily. Probably the Greek ear, trained on Homer's hexameters, was not impressed by the new and varied metres of the tragedians till the device was justified by being made the vehicle of great verse. The poet, like any other artist, has a right to resort to new devices to escape the outworn and conventional. But, now as before, he must show that they are both inspiring and controlling, not an obviously sophisticated addition of alloy, and still less a device for making base metal appear gold, but an alembic for fusing what is already gold into purer metal. Much poetic effort is rather a sort of elaborate hammering together of iron filings by ingenuity, not inspiration. The great poet is more apt to seek freedom in accepted forms than freedom from them, just as he is more apt to accept plots than to invent them. And in both cases he can afford to do so, because his imagination makes both new, with an individuality all its own, as we see in the difference of Homer's and Virgil's hexameters and Shakespeare's and Milton's pentameters.

Elaborate rhymes are still more doubtful, especially when handled with such difficulty that the rhyme does not help in finding the right word, as in Shelley or our best songs, but by its difficulty drives continually to contentment with the second best. Yet rhyme also is a strength to the master of it : and while neither metre nor rhyme makes poetry, some things printed even in anthologies of present writers, not only seem to lack both, but to be not very good prose cut up into lines of about equal length for no reason except not being very closely connected.

The essential quality of the poet is not to dissect things in his intellect but to see them whole in his imagination. He is of imagination all compact, which primarily is a way of seeing. The difference is like what Lawrence says of the French and English minds in *The Seven Pillars of Wisdom*. " Even in situations of poetry, the French remain incorrigibly prose writers ; seeing by the directly-thrown light of reason and under-standing, not through the half-closed eye, mistily by things' essential radiance, in the manner of the imaginative British." General conclusions about whole peoples are always hazardous, but these different ways of seeing are vital distinctions. Poetry is just seeing things by their essential radiance.

Yet it is thinking by seeing.

> Tell me where is fancy bred,
> Or in the heart or in the head.

Doubtless by gazing, yet if the eyes are not in a head which sees through them, it will certainly die in its cradle. And thinking through seeing may be much truer and more profound thinking than through ratio-cination. Nor is anyone a great poet who does not thus think, and what is more, see what is supremely worth thinking. The cutting may be what makes the perfect jewel, but only if expended on diamond of the first water not on paste.

We have already seen that the first essential of a true poet is a serious view of life, and that a serious view is in the end concerned neither with man's body nor his circumstances, nor even the superficial aspects of his mind. In the end it comes to his great moral decisions and his deep spiritual intuitions and aspirations. This is the essential insight of the penetrative imagination ; and the reason for turning to lust not love and the crude appetites and passions as a motive is lack, not merely of power to see the better, but of the resourceful imagination and fancy to make the better an inspiring theme. Even a true poet may have something of the coarseness of his age, but has he ever the animal or the seductive, or even in the deepest sense, the irreligious ?

As nearest to poetry we may pass to the essay. But just because of this nearness we need only ask what we take its distinguishing qualities to be. Obviously if we take the essayists accounted classical in English, such as Bacon, Addison, Lamb, Matthew Arnold, Emerson, there is vast variety : yet all alike seem to be marked by knowledge of life and sound and incisive judgment upon it, ingenuity of idea and felicity of expression, weighty thought concisely and memorably embodied, and the whole made genial by a kindly and easy manner. The smoothness of the essay is a defect in all public speech, but its felicity and compactness would save audiences from much empty verbiage.

Without further delay however we pass on to history, for it requires much fuller consideration.

Macaulay's *Essays* used to be the recognised gateway to the reading of history, for history was not a subject in the university curriculum when I was a student, and though there were one or two professors of it, even the historians of our time had not studied history in the

university. They gave their energies there to preparing
their tools, such as languages. The only beginning
possible, therefore, with history was interest : and
Macaulay managed to stir it in many young minds.
The kettledrums and cymbals in his style rather offended
the austerity of their taste, but it marched : and a
little inspiration from it might still help you to escape
colloquial flatness. His *History* has been described as
a huge Whig pamphlet. Yet it is not the maddening
sort of pamphleteering the War provided on all sides,
which first fixed the conclusion and then made the
evidence to fit it, but is a stout, hearty belief in his
own principles which could face up to any facts. Even
as prejudices, there is no difficulty in allowing for
them ; and in these days of harking back on authority,
they might be quite useful as an antidote. Yet while
you may begin with Macaulay, you may not rest
satisfied with him, because in the deepest concerns of
history he had little interest.

The question is what makes the true historian. The
ordinary reader has no dubiety, but the specialist is a
little given to thinking that the hodman is the architect.
Freeman was once thought accurate largely because he
was dull, and Froude inaccurate largely because he was
lively. About Froude's carelessness there is unfortunately no dubiety, but his dullness does not save Freeman
to-day from the same charge, even if in a less degree.
Gibbon wrote very brilliantly, but he is also phenomenally accurate. And there is no getting over the fact
that Froude, even if he had had no more regard for
facts than the Yellow Press, wrote in such a way that
he will continue to be read with pleasure, while Freeman,
had he been as accurate as a calculating machine, would
still have few readers and be likely to have fewer.

Thus Froude raises the question very sharply of
how far a historical work is to be judged as literature.
Not by this alone will it be justified, but also not without
it. There may have been persons in his time who
could, had they lived in ours, have won a better history

degree at Cambridge than Thucydides, but their work has not survived, and we shall continue to the end of time to think him the greatest Greek historian. Research has disposed of much that Livy took for fact, but the history of Rome lives in human imagination as he presented it. Though Carlyle was an extremely painstaking and accurate writer, research has found much to query in his *French Revolution*, but till someone writes a more brilliantly imaginative account of it, the ordinary English reader at least will continue to conceive it as he pictured it. And it will need a great writer as well as a great pundit to replace the account of the rise of the present situation in Europe in the first volume of *Frederick*.

His *Cromwell* raises another question. It is a speech against what he took to be a historical injustice—rather a plea than a presentation. Now how far may history be such a special plea, or wider still, a moral judgment? Certainly not in any way to interfere with a fair and balanced and proportionate statement of facts. For example, if it be true that Froude could not help being an advocate and an unfair one, it certainly would not add to his reputation as a historian. Yet is the entire absence of a moral judgment possible? For example, is Gardiner's *History of the Civil War*, with a little said on one side and a little on the other, the absence of a moral judgment, or a lame halting between two opinions? Is it not like a judge who has before him a case which is either right or wrong, but decides that it is six of the one and half a dozen of the other?

And this question may be widened. How far may a historian treat history as a background to his own view of life? Possibly he can do no other, however hard he try. And if you are to read history as a background to your own view of life, you can hardly quarrel with him for writing it as a background to his.

Even Gibbon, though he is the most learned and exact of historians, and is first and last just a historian,

is not free. And sometimes it means obvious prejudices. But obvious prejudices do not very much
mislead, and his work remains what has been described
as the great bridge from the old world to the new,
probably without rival in enabling you to look down
a long and in the main true historical perspective. His
style may be formal, but it maintains a level of distinction which, in so vast a work, is a high achievement.
Even by the time you have finished it you will probably
have forgotten a great deal more than you have remembered, but the present as well as the past will have a
larger meaning for you, and you will regard passing
events in a truer perspective. For example, is even so
vast a calamity as the last war to be compared with the
invasion of the barbarians ? And it may also help to
sustain the hope, that in spite of its autocracies, the
former, as the latter, is preparing a greater freedom.

History should give a large background to life : and
you should see life more clearly against it. So far as it
does this all history is revelation. Yet the Old and
New Testaments are singular among sacred literatures in
making use of it. That they present God's truth continuously against a background of history speaks of the
conviction that it is given in life, by life and for life.
Thereby this revelation is not the mere authority of the
past, but is experience to be tested by living experience.
In short it is revelation because it continues to be
revealing.

There may have been a specially sacred use made of
the Hebrew history but in itself it is no more sacred
than our own. If however you are to make good use
of any history you need to know life as well as history,
and it will never be a background to anything if it is
merely facts crammed up in youth. Perhaps it is not
a specially fitting study for youth at all, but ought to
be an increasing interest as the years bring you what
may often be the distressing as well as the widening
knowledge of men and things.

A professor of history in a confidential moment said,

" I am in the very unfortunate position of teaching a subject which I think ought not to be a university subject at all. At the university a man should develop his mind and learn his tools and master something he will not learn later : and for these purposes there is nothing still to beat the old subjects of Classics, Mathematics and Philosophy. History, on the other hand, a man should not seriously begin till he has fallen in love and had other even more disturbing experiences, so that he is not ignorant of the world and men. But then it may be the study of a lifetime, perhaps increasingly as his experience grows."

If so, it will not be so much remembering historical events as seeing a historical perspective that will be of value. Coleridge says that he had read libraries of historical books, and remembered next to nothing of them, yet his whole mind was composed of history.

What is known as 'Reading History' which is grinding at it in school from sixteen and throughout a university course, is too often only remembering what Coleridge forgot. Anyhow, if it is to do for you what it did for him, you must read the great histories. And the question is, What is a great history ? Size counts more than in most other branches of reading, because the small histories are apt to be mere potted facts, and second-hand at that. But while it is true, as Froude says, that the trouble about history is that it is usually a small man writing about a great one, a great history cannot be written by a small man, though he research day and night.

The greatest genius, it is true, could not write reliable history without research. And you ought to have some idea of what is historical proof, as you ought to have of what is scientific proof. But while any kind of research may be interesting amusement, for serious history only what would be important in the present can be important in the past. As 'important' mainly means what we can reconstruct in it of vital human interest, the historian needs imagination, as well as experience, even though he may not write imaginative history with the novelist's privilege of psychological omniscience.

Here is where the difficulty culminates. History cannot tell us what happened, but only what it can prove happened, and this may have as much life as a fossil unless it rests on some kind of eye-witness. Then comes the further difficulty of cross-examining it.

Ranke, the historian of the Papacy, tells how his interest in historical evidence was first stirred by receiving entirely different versions of an accident from different eye-witnesses within an hour of its happening. It used to be thought that only time produced myth. But, when put in the cold storage of indifferent memory, narratives change little, while, fermenting in the minds of those keenly interested, and perhaps with their own reputation at stake they can suffer a sea change in a very short time. For example, few sources will be more perplexing for the future historian of the late war than the many narratives of those who bore a leading part in it.

For this reason, while autobiographies are often extremely interesting, most of them are what Goethe named his, *Truth and Phantasy*. Journals may be more immediate, or records of conversation such as Luther's or Wesley's, or Eckermann's *Conversations of Goethe*. But even then you have to realise the personal element in the recorder.

The best biographies are those which make their subject speak for themselves, such as Boswell's *Johnson*. Just because human life should be one of your supreme interests, biography should have an important place in your reading. But even in the most interesting biographies you will often have to make allowance for the biographer. Moreover, biographies live by form as well as substance. For example, all Wilson's laborious research will not probably replace Froude's *Carlyle*, even though he proves up to the hilt how much Froude's whole narrative is distorted, because, alas, he could not write like Froude.

M

Novels are a kind of literature peculiarly subject to change of interest. Richardson once had an immense vogue, but how many could wade through one of his works to-day ? Fielding was a great novelist, but to read him you must brace yourself a good deal more than, for example, for Edgar Wallace. At one time people read George Eliot with breathless interest. To-day the few who are still interested in the work of a very able mind are rather calm and critical than enthusiastic. Dickens and Thackeray are, I understand, setting suns, and the sun of a good many very popular novelists of a later date is already set. The question is, how far should we acquiesce ? Unfortunately only Scott's very Scottish novels are really good. But there is a healthy open-air humanity about *The Antiquary*, *Guy Mannering*, *Rob Roy*, *The Heart of Midlothian* and *Old Mortality*, in which many still continue to find relief from our more introspective age, and which one can hardly conceive that the world will commit to oblivion. Dickens is of even more varied quality. But *David Copperfield* is surely as immortal as such literature can be, if only because Mr Micawber is better known to us than Burleigh and Betsy Trotwood more real than Queen Elizabeth. And there are still a few sufficiently un-sophisticated to enjoy the humour of Pickwick. Carlyle said of Thackeray, " There is no one among us writing English like him. He is a big man, but he is not as strong as he is big." This is true criticism. But it is something to be a big man, and few qualities give immortality like a perfect style, and no one has invented anyone more diabolically clever than Becky Sharp, nor written anything so finished as *Esmond*. And what is to be said of the taste which revives Trollope and neglects Meredith ?

Taine charges the English novel, and to some extent all English literature, with the inveterate and pernicious habit of preaching, and contrasts it unfavourably with Balzac's acceptance of men and things just as they are. But the difference again may be between seeing only with the directly-thrown light of intellect and seeing by the essential radiance with the half-closed eye of the imagination.

You must I suppose glance at the newspaper. The question is how much, and at what time of the day. Certainly not newspapers and little else, and not in the best hours of the morning. Periodical literature you should take in very small doses, but perhaps you should have at least one literary journal. The rise of ephemeral productions, to which the readers expect to give no more than a fleeting interest and not to remember at all, struck Goethe with dismay, as only fitted to blur the mind and distract and dissipate living interests. And his fear has not proved groundless.

Finally there is miscellaneous reading, reading which happens to interest you. As there can be no other standard of this than your own taste, there is little use in making suggestions. In this taste, have by all means the utmost catholicity, even if it be not always of the highest. You will not be much of a reader at all unless you read a great many books just because you find yourself in a mood to read them. Yet you should never become a mere indiscriminating swallower of books.

XVIII

WRITING

WRITING, properly done, should certainly help to make you exact men. But might it not also help to make you ready men and full men ?

One kind of readiness writing only too easily imparts, which is to produce stuff to fire off at a moment's notice. At a conference a bright spirit will be on his feet, making deliverance of finalities on the weightiest points of principle or policy, while his neighbour has scarce begun to ponder the difficulties. Presently you suspect the resurrection of a letter which was to set right the times, had not the organ which claims to reflect them been smitten with blindness ; or a pamphlet which was to create a new heaven and a new earth, had not the writer failed to find faith in the world of publishers. It may even be so amazingly complete and confident as to suggest the youthful omniscience of a class essay. Or the facile command of clichés in embattled series may indicate a more recent effort of prophetic anticipation of what might be wanted, as near to the speaker's heart as the inside breast-pocket of his coat. Copious pious phraseology still more indicates the facile pen, and makes you more than ever wish that a chairman could be as unhampered by politeness as an editor. Most of all in religious controversy, the most learned man who ever lived—all the more because he is learned and knows how much knowledge is limited—is easily outshone by one who, from little controversial handbooks, has written out for himself neat, pointed, dogmatic answers. And the same is apt to be true of examinations. The student with extensive first-hand knowledge, from which he cannot merely reproduce but has to select what is relevant and ponder his selection anew before he can give it form, often makes a poor show compared with one who has in readiness second-hand knowledge done up neatly in parcels from his note-books.

Even when the pen is not thus a labour-saving device for not knowing and not thinking, but has been used for its legitimate purpose of making clear your thought and ordering your knowledge, it may still take the spontaneous verve out of human intercourse. More perhaps than is generally recognised, what seems even to the speaker himself unprepared utterance may depend on what, at some time, he has written. Yet of the spontaneity which is an essential of interesting human intercourse, there is at least a passable imitation so long as he is not a conscious plagiarist from his own compositions.

My old professor of English used to picture Ben Jonson in conversation as like a Spanish galleon, and Shakespeare playing round him like an English frigate. In spite of his ready wit, Shakespeare may not have felt bound to reject a telling hit because it was somewhere in his writings. But he would, I think, be trying to forget that he had ever put pen to paper, while the illustrious Ben would, probably, be always trying to recall the wise and witty sayings he had laboriously manufactured at his desk. Possibly, however, he carried it off like the professor himself, who, though the description had been given from a way-worn manuscript with verbal exactness to many generations of students, always managed to deliver it as though it had occurred to him at the moment, because, somehow, he could convince himself that it had. If this was not readiness, it was an extremely plausible substitute.

Writing would also go far to help to make you full men, if to write things down impressed them upon the memory in proportion to the faith of the devotees of the note-book. The patient labour at taking copious notes of lectures and making long extracts and abstracts from books is a work of faith, but it is not a work that justifies the faith.   The student whose notes are mere jottings finds them a challenge to memory and keeps most of what he learns in lectures, but the man who makes them a substitute for memory, very little. Memory, like other servants, is most reliable when most trusted.   There is truth in the ancient Greek saying that the gods gave men writing and took away memory.

Many note-books are filled in the belief that merely to have anything in them is to know it.   But there is a saying of Quintilian which runs somewhat like this : *Tantum scimus quantum in memoria tenemus :* and it means that we know it nowhere else.   The view of many students, however, is rather *Tantum scimus quantum in libello memoriale scribimus.*   And in this way no doubt are produced the learned books which conserve in foot-notes every triviality that was ever written on the subject, as William James says, ' like flies in amber.' When an author tells you that his method of producing a book is first to draw up a list of authorities, then, after disembowelling them, to order and index the result, whereupon little remains except the mechanical task of writing, you understand why, having read one of his books, you never wish to see another.

Though unfortunately not with the same inspired result, my own experience rather accords with Stevenson's.   No reading, he said, or no experience was of much use to him while it was still new and raw, but had, before he could use it, to be kept and mellowed in memory like wine in a cask.   And the reason is simple.   Knowledge in a note-book is at best stored ; knowledge in the memory is always transforming itself and your mind with it.   It is not merely in your minds, but is your active minds themselves. Wherefore it is Quintilian's saying that is true, and writing is not a substitute and only a very unreliable support.

This activity of memory no doubt also has its drawbacks, because what remains emotionally active in the

memory is apt to change. Wherefore, though immediately written records are of value, you ought to cross-
question what you think you know very closely before you
write, because personal interest can pervert perception as
well as recollection.

This might be an argument for keeping a diary.
Being incapable of such sustained effort, I have no
means of judging. Without it the task of trying to
recover how you thought of life many years ago certainly
seems hopeless. But probably you would not have
known any better if you had written it down at the
time. Moreover, the reason why one cannot recall what
manner of person he was may be lack of interest in
himself, which was probably a quite profitable indifference. What did interest him he will probably still see
pretty clearly, possibly too with a finer truth, in looking
back along the whole vista of events, than any diary
could conserve. And in addition only when so seen
could it be known what was worth recording. Had
Goethe kept a diary, he might have had fewer slips in
facts, but could he have given as clear and illuminating
a picture of a great and stirring time as he did with his
unaided memory ?

This leads us to the main question of how to write
so as to be more exact, for this is certainly not the effect
of every kind of writing.

No aim should be so central in writing as exactness.
Yet this requires discrimination of the kind of exactness
to be desired, because it does not mean that you must
always be defining your terms or never make a statement
without safeguarding its precision with a parenthesis.
Good writing is not a legal document, which assumes
the utmost perversity and even hostility in its readers,
but appeals to their sympathy and willingness to do
their best to understand. And preaching in particular
is of no value till it has created this atmosphere of
mutual accord.

You are not to tax the forbearance of your hearers
more than you can help : and to this end it is well

to exercise yourself in other ways of writing than composing sermons.

Writing poetry is the severest discipline. You need not inflict the result upon your friends, but if you feel like trying and can lift it above doggerel, it is worth while persisting.

The next best perhaps is translation. But first of all you must learn that it is not to be done merely by selecting equivalent words from the dictionary. Words in different languages seldom have exactly the same connotation. Nor may you resort to the easy device of paraphrasing. Nor should the result be merely foreign idiom in English words. But if you first think precisely through what the writer says in his own tongue, and then try to express it exactly in your own, you will discover the amazing resources of the English language, so that, when you fail, you will not be ready to accept any excuse except your own imperfect mastery of it. Poetry in the strict sense is untranslatable, but there is some good in trying, because even a faint approach to the impossible may teach you more than easy achievement.

But however you see good to practise the art, the first requirement, if it is to make you exact men, is to have your loins girt and your lamp burning, to concentrate, and that on a clearly-seen purpose. The danger of extempore speaking is just lack of exactness, rambling on with fluent diffuseness : but in face of an audience with the criticism of bored faces confronting you, the danger can never be so great as of extempore writing with no resentment from the paper on which it is inflicted.

In preparation for speaking, you have probably been told that you ought to write as you would speak. But unless you write a great deal more exactly than you can speak, writing is worse than waste of time. You will lose in freedom and force, and if you cannot make up for the loss by felicity, condensation and order, writing is an extremely profitless occupation. The

most appalling state into which anyone may fall is
to be driven to blacken so many sheets of paper from
sheer terror of being gravelled from lack of vocables.
Even nonsense is not so intolerable uttered impromptu
as when obviously deliberately perpetrated in writing
and recited.

As writing should be for making exact your thought,
it is a gain that you cannot write as fast as you can
speak and of doubtful advantage to quicken the process,
be it by contractions, omissions, short-hand, or even
the typewriter, seeing that you will probably be able to
write in full as fast as you can think to profit. Short-
hand in particular may be useful in putting down other
people's thought, or possibly your own on occasion, but
is of less than no value for chastening your own. Those
who use it seem to be in danger of adding as tags to
their sentences phrases which, had their medium not
been so easy, they would have had time to put in as one
fitting word in its right place in the middle. Having
sprained my thumb diving in shallower water than I
expected, I was driven for a time to use a typewriter.
Some people it is said use a typewriter, not because it
writes faster, but because they like to hear themselves
think. My trouble, on the contrary, was that from its
meaningless chatter in my ear I could not hear myself
think. Indeed I rather came to feel that it had a
prejudice against thinking, in contrast with my old
silent and unobtrusive friend the pen, which not only
did not interfere with any thinking I was able to do, but,
unlike the modern babbling invention, had at times a
spirit of divination of what I wanted to say.

The only question is whether the pen is not too easy
and paper too cheap. Think of sitting down with a
stylus before an expensive papyrus or vellum, and how
you would weigh each word before you made it stare
at you in bold uncials upon the precious page. Even
wax tablets would be an encouragement to think before
you wrote, and not trust that your thought would
somehow come out at the point of your pen, especially

in days when melting it out was not made easy by the invention of matches.

Each person has his own way of writing at his best, and you should discover what is yours. One person composes, in the sense of consciously putting his work together ; another has to fuse it into unity in his mind as in the melting-pot, with writing merely as pouring it into the mould. Yet the best writing probably always had first this fusing in the fire of imagination and interest, however much afterwards it may have been finished cold with the critical judgment. Some evidence of this you will find in the manuscripts of authors. For example there are two copies of *In Memoriam* in the Cambridge Trinity Library, the first and the final writing. There are many emendations in the latter, but the former is astonishingly perfect. The mere neat and characteristic handwriting of most great writers also speaks of the previous mastery of what they are writing.

Though you may learn from the emendations that it is quite easy to change for harm and not good, few I fancy have been satisfied wholly with their first achievement.

From Ben Jonson's description, it is apparent that Shakespeare wrote rapidly at white heat, and some of his plays seem to have been left untouched. But you can hardly suppose that a play like Othello, for example, was made so perfect in every word at one throw even of his mind. Milton tells us of how his thoughts in harmonious numbers moved, before he wrote or dictated them. Yet all his poems suggest the finishing hand of the careful sculptor. Ruskin says it was his habit to write rapidly and revise slowly. Froude states that Carlyle at his best made no foul copy : but his latest biographer materially modifies this statement by letting us know that the revision of the proof-sheets was a terror to the printer. No writing will march merely by composing and correcting : but also no labour is wasted which orders its ranks with more exactness.

As you go on in life this aim in writing, to make it the exact expression of exact thinking, may not grow easier. Let us hope indeed that you will find it increasingly difficult, for if not you have probably not persevered in it. When the fire of imagination and the force of youth grow less, the smelting of your thought is a slower process. Then one of two things happens to you. As your creative faculty decays your critical continues to grow, and you produce with ever-increasing difficulty and ever-diminishing satisfaction. Should this distress you, go and hear the brother who has landed in the other situation, which is the decay of the critical faculty along with the creative. When you see how he rejoices in having acquired the pen of a ready writer, unhampered by any doubt of the quality of what it produces, you can go home and thank the Lord that if your stuff is bad, He still permits you to know it is bad. Then when you sit down to write and find that

> Surely the golden hours are turning grey
> And dance no more and vainly strive to run,

you may even be thankful for the invention of cursive script to make smoother their halting steps, and that paper is cheap to diminish the temptation to say with Pilate, "What I have written I have written." Fortunately the waste-paper basket denies that it is necessarily true that *literae scriptae manent*, and it may be well from the beginning not to sorrow much over its kindly oblivion. At any time when you are quite satisfied, it may be well to think of Thorwaldsen weeping over his last statue, and when asked if he were not satisfied, replying that as he saw no fault in it, he knew that his imagination was in decay.

You may find that, having been students first and preachers perhaps long afterwards, writing had become your natural form of expressing yourselves before you have even attempted to address an audience, and that you can hardly ever hope to become on the same easy terms with your public as with your paper, which, if your organ is to be the pulpit and not the press, may be a severe handicap.

Might this not show that the order should be reversed, and public speech be exercised before writing? But while in theory it should be possible to acquire freedom first and exactness afterwards, in practice it is extremely unusual. A frequent commendation of candidates for the ministry is that they have already astonishing fluency of public speech. Sad experience has caused us to expect not merely a wind-bag, but one so full of wind that we can never hope to get anything else into him. Glib utterance of conventional ideas and familiar phrases, unfortunately, commands an earlier popularity than groping after truth and hesitating utterance of it by the thoughtful man who can say only what he knows and feels. But if it grow up like Jonah's gourd, it also withers like it, while the other may increase in influence for a lifetime. As this enduring influence is our concern here, the way of freedom first and exactness afterwards is not open for our consideration. Moreover, the day when copious conventional utterance was acceptable seems to be passing: while the man who has something worth saying and says it with increasing simplicity, clearness and precision, still finds a hearing. At the same time you will be severely handicapped, and especially in what you ought to do like your Master, in preaching the gospel to the poor, unless to exactness you add freedom. This raises the question of how far and in what way is writing directly of profit for preaching.

You can of course write out your sermon fully and follow your manuscript closely. And there have been great and impressive preachers who were close readers. Dr Chalmers was spoken of as a 'fell reader.' Newman moved Oxford by his preaching, and through Oxford a much wider audience, though he scarcely lifted his eyes from his paper. Martineau I believe argued that a sermon ought to be a finished product in form and substance, and therefore should be written out fully and read closely. But, in most people's hands at least, there would be the danger of being icy without being regular, and null without being splendid. Even of the most powerful read sermons can you say more than that, if there is sufficient force and conviction and personal quality, it will break through anything? You would need to be sure that you possess them, before you could afford to do without the opener road of looking your audience in the face and acquiring, at least in some measure, the freer forms of conversational speech.

One device for uniting the exactness of writing with freedom of speech is what was called in the old days 'mandating,' that is committing your manuscript to heart. And this also can be done successfully. For example I rather suspect Cicero of the practice. And if you have, like him, a spacious oratorical style, it is probably not excessively difficult. But if you cherish simplicity of language, have acquired the habit of condensation, and perhaps indulge yourself in antithesis, you will probably find your eyes still farther from your audience, and still more at the back of your head trying to see the word you have written, than you would following your manuscript even pretty closely.

Speaking from a manuscript, whether read or remembered, is like following the turnpike; speaking from few notes or none is like keeping your eye on the goal and taking the hedges and ditches as they come and as best you can. They are not merely different practices, but involve different attitudes of mind, which are hard to unite at least in one effort. Therefore a mixture of both methods is, for most people at least, worst of all.

Yet there is a right sense in which you should write as you would speak. While your writing ought to be more exact than you can speak without its aid, your

style in writing should have the freedom and ease of
movement of good speaking, and the same geniality.
You cannot have too much concentration, but you
should not seek it by knitting the brows and scowling
and hitting out. The servant of the Lord should not
strive in writing any more than in speaking. Nor
should you write in an unnatural, stilted, inverted
way, any more than you should speak. Some people's
pens seem to have been brought up in the schools of
the scribes to write antiquely and to write backwards.
No sentence is esteemed of proper literary quality
unless its subject is where it might not be expected,
and no word of due artistic quality unless it has ceased
from common usage, ancient adverbs, like 'albeit' and
'erstwhile,' giving the same satisfaction as putting
up *Ye olde Englishe Hostelrie*, on an aggressively
modern inn.

Yet however clearly, simply, forcibly, modernly you
learn to write, the ministry will be a drudgery, and a
dull one at that, unless you acquire some command of
freedom of speech. The choice moreover will come to
be between extempore speaking and extempore writing.
Then, if you have to swim on bladders of improvised
writing, your writing will be apt to degenerate into
emptier, flatter utterance than could ever be achieved
in face of your fellows.

You cannot have less natural gift for free speech than
I had, nor possibly receive less encouragement to try.
One friend said, "It is no use. Your written word
seldom lacks character, your spoken word has none."
Another said, "What on earth took you to-day? I heard
your voice certainly, but not one word that was yours."
I saw that if I continued to write every word I had
to utter, the writing would soon be as much without
character as the speaking. Wherefore, though it tried
the long-suffering of the audience and distressed myself,
I persisted. As these talks may show, the result still is
nothing to boast of, yet even they might lose some
quality by being written.

If you write with any degree of care, you may find yourselves helpless without your manuscript, but if you have clearly before you where you hope to arrive, and use notes only to indicate the turnings and perhaps the concrete word you want where you are in danger of diverging into abstractions, you will get along without stumbling, and the fewer notes, even to none, the smoother the passage. Though some may still prefer the written discourse, there will be more whom you could never reach at all if you do not achieve some more conversational and direct form of address. The preparation will not necessarily be easier, nor will it always take less time, but there is a gain to oneself in having more than one method, and a marked increase of the possibility of not writing except with the aim of greater exactness. Your notes, if you use any, should not be general statement of your line of thought, which should be in your head and before you all the time, but the concrete and if possible the picturesque word, and suggestions regarding transitions from one point to another.

Each person has his own most helpful method, and there is no rule applicable to all cases. Yet as most ministers write both too copiously and too carelessly, it might be good advice to write, at not too long intervals, to meet your own highest critical standard. And, if you have done it sufficiently exactly, to attempt to do without your manuscript will probably only lead to halting and hesitating for the right word. The result will probably not be your most popular effort, and very likely not your most edifying. But all your other speaking will benefit, in order, in fitness of word and phrase, in short in exactness, and even your most casual utterance may be saved from being mere rambling on from one point to another in an exhaustless flow of commonplace verbosity. Though preaching should not be a mere manufacture at your desk, even the prophets gave their message form by writing ; and you are not likely to need its discipline less. Only let it be discipline of what already possesses your souls, not a device to provide words to be a substitute for inspiration. Let their example too remind you that prophecy is distinguished from frenzy, precisely by the fact that it can be expressed in few, simple, sincere, precise words, which may have beauty as well as exactness.

XIX

PREPARATION AND PROGRESS

THAT preaching ought to be a by-product of your whole life does not mean that you have only to be good people and your sermons will be good on their own, in glorious independence of the primal curse that " in the sweat of thy face shalt thou eat bread." Right living, for the preacher as for other men, is turning this curse into a blessing. By-products do not just happen of themselves. Glycerine, I think I have heard, is a by-product of soap, but apparently it took much knowledge and skill to discover that it was not a mere noxious ingredient. Many valuable chemicals are a by-product of smelting iron, but they merely polluted the atmosphere till, after much thought and experiment, a furnace was invented that captured them. Your study should be such a smelting furnace for capturing the inspirations from all life's drab experiences, and it requires much skilled experiment, as well as labour, to make it effective.

It has been solemnly argued that time spent in preparing sermons is mere disobedience to the counsel, " Take no thought beforehand what ye shall speak," and distrust in the promise that the Spirit will, when the time comes, give you what to say. And the argument is clenched in the manner of our old friend Euclid : if this be so when you stand before governors and kings, how much more when you are facing only ordinary people ! And it must be a very old idea that true piety should do no thinking, because a scribe soon after added, " Neither do ye premeditate " to the original saying, " Be not anxious beforehand."

Apart from the crude idea that the Spirit's aid is not

N   193 to help us to think to better purpose, but to save us the trouble of loving God with all our minds, can anyone suppose that Paul's very finished speeches before Felix and Festus had never been premeditated, though it is plain that he would not have been so calmly master of the situation had he been distressed by previous anxiety. So far is taking thought, in the sense of worrying, from real thinking, that it is thinking's worst enemy.

While premeditation might not be of much profit if you were set before governors and kings, whose acquaintance you make for the first time and in situations you cannot predict, it does not follow that, for people you do know and teaching which you are aware is needed, you have the same right to depend on the inspiration of the moment, and not wait on the Spirit after a fashion more active as well as more patient. And this is apart from the fact that the woman who was a sinner may be a more important person in God's eyes and a much more hopeful case for your care than that fox Herod.

With what is quite uncertain, the time to expect help for the right word is when the event requires it, and troubling your mind beforehand is not only waste of time, but the worst possible preparation. As it cannot be foreseen, it does not belong to to-day's evils, with which alone you are to be concerned. But if it is for teaching and edifying known people in a known situation, even though you may not be called upon till Sunday, the preparation for it may be to-day's evil, and this at a much earlier day in the week than Saturday. If our Lord's answers to Pilate do not seem to have been premeditated, you cannot say the same about His parables or the Sermon on the Mount even granted that it may be, as we have it, collected from many sermons. Teaching in parables appears to have been a method He found in use and merely perfected, but He took the trouble to perfect it as had never been done before. Even if the parables came to Him at the time, they were the outcome of His whole intercourse with men and His reading of Scripture, perhaps all His reading, and of much meditation on how most vividly and clearly to impress the truth upon men's minds. Some have even thought that His preaching shows signs that much of it was originally in poetic form. Anyhow there is much in it of the deliberate parallelism of the Psalter, which is one of the reasons why it is so memorable. Jesus was a teacher who 'waited upon His teaching,' concerned not only with what He said but also with how to say it in the way most profitable to His hearers.

But while 'Take no thought' is very far from 'Do no thinking,' there may still be very unprofitable thinking, and very unprofitable care to dress up second-class thought in first-class language, or, what is worse, to use stately language to obscure the absence of any serious thinking.   Even short of this, it might only result in a kind of mechanical manufacture.

A practical method of helping yourselves out in time of need is to keep a commonplace book, and to collect in it all you read and hear that you think good in itself and likely to be helpful. If you have a memory which can do without it, so much the better. It would plainly be superfluous if you could refer to any page of a book you have read. But if you have not, you may find " a commonplace book," as Fuller puts it, " contains notions in garrison, whence the owner may draw out an army into the field." You must, however, have a high standard of recruiting, if a commonplace book in the ancient sense of what is of general value is not to degenerate into a book of commonplaces in the modern sense.

The value of such a garrison will still depend on your own way of working, and your power of drawing it out as an army in the field on the extent to which you are a methodical person.

Different methods of writing have already been mentioned. Pope, who composed in the sense of putting things together, was probably very dependent on such collecting ; while it is unlikely that Shakespeare, with his way of writing, ever kept notes of metaphors or the characteristics of human nature, or could have made such use of them if he had.

Even if you should need such aid, however, unless you have persistence in making it and order in using it, it will not be a very present help.   Thus though I might encourage you by precept, it might be honest to confess that it is not by example.   However much in need of such help, I have never had the order and patience necessary for such an undertaking; and being a very unmethodical person, I should never have been able to find in it what was wanted.   Even a quotation never seems to occur to me unless it turn up on its own in a casual way.

In the end you come to what you can yourselves produce.

Fertility of course is a native gift, yet even a very fertile person like Goethe evidently found it an inter-mittent spring, for we find this in his *Conversations* :— " As Meyer always says, ' If thinking were not so hard.' But the worst is that the very hardest thinking will not bring thoughts.   They must come like good children of God and cry, ' Here we are.' "   Yet neither do they come unsought, but are like what William James says of memories.   You try your hardest to recover them. Then, after you have given up, they come sauntering in with their hands in their pockets, though if the effort had not opened the door to them, they would not have come.

How then are you to keep them when they do come ?

> We cannot kindle when we will
> The fires that in the heart reside,
> The Spirit bloweth and is still,
> In solitude our hearts abide.
> But tasks in hours of insight willed
> Can be through hours of gloom fulfilled.

One of the greatest gifts in life is to be able to capture the bright moments, teach by them, learn from them, apply them, and then find them shining in the dull days brighter than before.   Most effectively this comes to pass as they become a living creative interest in the

memory, yet as they so often escape with no other
security, cannot something more be done to preserve
them ?

Many great thoughts have been given to the world
which were just jotted down when they came and how
they came, which would have been lost had the writers
waited for what might have appeared to them a more
convenient season or a better order. Pascal's *Pensées*
were just such jottings, and the fragments of Novalis
the same. To some also such early notes have been
germs of most of their best later work, as for example
Carlyle, in whose notebook hints of nearly all he afterwards developed are to be found. Thackeray, I think it
was, who felt it so important to catch the first glow of a
thought, the ' first fine careless rapture,' that he would
get up in the middle of the night to put it down.
Whether our bright visions of the night would look less
drab than they have a habit of doing in the morning
light, if we defied discomfort and seized opportunity by
the forelock, would with each of us need to be tried
out to learn. Yet only if you put down your thoughts
rapidly, almost unreflectingly, eager only to catch the
moment's feeling and impulse, thus imprisoning them,
as it were, only in wires and not in walls, will your note-
book be a cage for singing birds and not a tomb for
dead ones.

Even in notes for sermons, though every one must
work out his own method, it is probably sound advice to
most of you to keep a note of texts and divisions and
ideas and illustration of them, or even a mere title, or
at all events, in reading your Bible, to indicate possible
subjects, and put a note or two on the margin of how
you might treat them. For one thing it keeps a number
of subjects before your minds : and then it is wonderful
how they unfold themselves, even without much thinking, till some day they fit into a mood, and you have
your sermon almost ready. Even some small suggestion
may be sufficient to start the whole crystallisation of
your thought.

There may come times when you cannot, by any effort, lift your message above the level of the commonplace, or you may not even have time or energy to try. How far it may be profitable then to use another person's sermon, with frank acknowledgment of its origin, you can only say after trying. But another person's work would need to be very much better than your own to be equally effective ; and to be much more impressively delivered, which is just what you probably could not do. If therefore the worst comes to the worst, it is better to fall back on your own past work.

This practice may also have some justification for its own sake. Persons have been heard of who, when they changed their sphere, burned their old sermons to deliver them from the temptation of using them again. The reason given is the amazing rate at which they outgrow themselves, so that they would have to descend from the heights to their effort of even a year ago. Unfortunately the progress is seldom as apparent to others, which is natural enough, as the true reason for the belief is lack of critical judgment of what is still hot from the oven.

The sermons of your maturer years will, let us hope, also be maturer ; but they may not be better for certain purposes, or always better in any sense. You have young hearers as well as old, and your youthful work may mean more to them just because it is youthful. But also, if you have any inspiration at all, subjects will stir your interest in certain situations or appeal to some mood or experience, so that you will think them out more clearly and present them more vividly than you will ever be able to do again in all your lives. Shakespeare, for example, could not have written *Lear* when he wrote *As You Like It*, but neither could he have written *As You Like It* when he wrote *Lear*. And the same is true of Milton's *Allegro* and *Samson*. How much would have been lost had Milton been so impressed by his own development in *Paradise Lost* that he resolved to burn all that had been written before, or even to alter it according to his new standard of excellence. Some products of special moments of insight you may have from youth to age : and so far from destroying them, you should use them again without altering much, even in their form. Moreover you ought to try to recapture the mood in which you wrote them, which itself will help to keep you young, and you will be delivered from the real difficulty of preaching old sermons, which is not being able to recover their inspiration. Anyhow, even if you never use them again, they are probably the best record of your own thought and ways of thinking that you could produce.

We sometimes hear of a technique of sermon making, which seems to be a special art over and above the ordering of thought necessary for addressing any audience. It sounds like a process of manufacture, whereas a sermon should be, in some dim sense at least, a creation. To say that God created the heavens and the earth and all that is therein does not mean that, like the old image of Him modelling them with brawny arms out of clay, He manufactured them. The difficulty with manufacture is breathing into it the breath of life.

There is no doubt something of a technique in writing poetry, but the poet who first constructed it, and then manufactured his poetry according to it, would not have a very inspired result. Nor would one technique ever meet his need, if his genius have any range. After the work is done, the critics may discover a technique, but it is improbable that the poet was conscious of it like the critic. Thus it has been thought that the date of Shakespeare's plays can be determined by the development of his metre, but probably it would have been information for Shakespeare himself. In any case, it is one thing to discover the technique which best embodies a varied inspiration, and another to start with it as a fixed mode of operation.

If you do so, you may produce a very finished article, but a monotonous one, like the artists who make a hit

with birch-trees or children playing on the sands or
sunsets over the sea, and go on repeating the effect
with mere changes of the set pieces.

At the same time, both the poet and the artist have
rules and standards determined for them, at once by
the medium in which they work and the result they
wish to achieve.

The end which seems to have been common to all
the great artists and great poets, was to sing their
way into the soul of man, the common soul that was
made in the image of God and whose understanding
was from the inspiration of His spirit, and could be
moved by what stirred this inspiration.   Therefore,
however much they might give it individual character,
there was common to the poets the medium of exact
and fine and melodious words, expressing a progress of
thought which could justify itself to the intellect, while
having a deeper order which stirred the heart, embodied in what was common experience, yet exalted to
the elemental and the eternal by the ' vision and the
faculty divine.'   And the artists sought the same end
by means of colour and arrangement, interpreting and
fixing the beautiful and sublime but fleeting moments
of nature and the deepest thought and feeling as they
pass over the faces of men when peace had spread her
wings over them or when they rose to sublime heights
of action.

On the uses of their media by some modern poets and
artists, it may be lack of education which makes me
think them crude, but I cannot help the feeling that
they are bizarre.   Now the bizarre is not intended to
sing its way, but to batter its way into the human soul,
and however much you may profess to despise those
who do not succumb, you cannot really respect those
who do.

In any case the preacher's business is not with the
elect, in the sense of the select, but with man as man,
and with the right direction of his common thoughts
and the right deciding of his common ways ; and to

this end he should sing his way, with simple truth and the beauty of holiness into the human soul, and not attempt to batter his way through by any device of mere vehemence or startling paradox.

Wherefore, just as the poets and the artists have common methods and forms, so have preachers. A sermon should have a logical order and a spiritual; it should have a beginning, a middle and an end; if it have a text, this should be a key-note and not an abstraction; there should be a case to win before the intellect and a practical end to be accepted by the conscience: and this should be done by the medium of felicitous and memorable speech and life's commonest experience, lifted out of the ordinary and commonplace and exalted into the elemental and spiritual.

Just because this must remain inspiration and can never be fashioned into the mechanical regularity of a technique, no discussion of it can be adequate. Nevertheless some direction of our minds to it, however imperfect, may not be wholly unprofitable.

You may not assume, merely because you are full of your subject, that you have only to say to your thoughts 'Stand not upon the order of your going.' Vast erudition and enthusiasm for detail have produced speeches like an antiquarian shop without a catalogue, where treasures and trifles are mixed in hopeless confusion. All the more, therefore, if your interest be comprehensive and your knowledge extensive, selection and order may be necessary.

Saying many things is seldom saying much. 'A stream of rapid talk with nothing in it,' and 'There is three times as much in it as people need' seem opposites in form, but may be perfectly consistent criticisms in substance, for it is the development of one truth, in all its depth and height, that is real thinking, and not throwing up one point after another, like a juggler tossing balls.

Just for the development of one idea a plan is necessary. Yet thinking out the plan will develop your thought only if the plan is your own. According to the old tag *dispositio* aids *inventio*, if it be what Hegel calls 'the labour of the notion.' But the better another person's plan is, if you simply adopt it, the more likely you are to be left wondering how you could do so little with what promised so much.

As students you may be too easily satisfied merely with connected and consistent thinking, like gardeners who think more of the straightness of their rows than of the quality of their seed. Better good seed sown broadcast, if scattered abroad from the hopper, with each seed still having room, not emptied in heaps from the sack. Yet a logical order is making sure of this by, as it were, planting each seed with the dibble in its own place.

Though this should help you to rise, in Milton's sense, to the height of your great argument, it should not be argumentative. Few things are more annoying than to hear an opponent's arguments put in a way that makes them too absurd for discussion and then disposed of with a flourish of trumpets. Even good argument is seldom of profit in the pulpit, but if you feel called to enter upon it, be sure that what you say is convincing and not merely ingenious. Your own cleverness may convince yourself, while it merely raises distrust in the minds of other people. The only helpful logical order is one that makes plain your line of progress and enables your hearer to march along with you in the confidence that you are advancing along one road in one direction.

There is a higher sequence than the logical, what we might call the moral, an order according to the appeal to the heart and the conscience. But it is just as a skeleton for this living order that a logical order is most necessary, because, without it, the appeal to the heart is apt to be mere vapid sentiment and almost physical emotion, and to the conscience mere vague stirring of the desire to be good and do good, which sets no one forward on a clear and upward path, but is merely a sort of turning to the east to say one's prayers as the only element of supplication.

Nevertheless any logical order you may have ought to be the handmaid of this higher order of persuasion. With this before you you should begin, and not your sermon only but your whole service.

A good many people have come to church merely as their custom is. This may not be the highest reason, but do not be too superior to consider it, for it is a very good reason. Our Lord Himself went to the synagogue on the Sabbath, as His custom was. Even He did not despise the support of good customs. In our restless time any custom of church attendance might be profitable to body and spirit. But, as always happens with mere custom, it is in decay when most needed. All the more therefore, so far as it continues, your business is to meet it and lead it farther, that what is merely a custom may become a privilege. Even where there is the highest motive, you must still remember that the devoutest mother of a family has had a flurried time setting her household in order and making her flock presentable, and even if her husband is one of your most religious office-bearers, after a very hard week he may have just been resting from it or even still worried with it. Both have come hoping to be interested in something higher, and this is all you have a right to ask of them : and you must start with them where they are and gently lure them on. A service which starts with shouting " Onward Christian Soldiers," and ends with muttering drowsily " I will both lay me down in peace and sleep," is of the nature of an anti-climax. Nor should you expect a general audience to be down in the depths any more than up in the heights.

One lovely summer morning I wished to start with one of the most sombre of metrical psalms, " My days are like a shade alway, which doth declining swiftly pass." The organist, who had a fine full-blooded stammer, which gave peculiar emphasis to his speech said, " Do you sup-pose that the p-people will want to come in out of the b-bright s-sunshine to s-sing that?" It was sound criticism. Even if it be the minor chords of the heart which in the end you would touch to music, you must still take up your congregation where most of them are, neither down in the depths nor up in the clouds, but in what you might call a depressed yet dogged hopefulness. To this mood an all right with the world sort of tone will seem a denial that their struggle is real and an all wrong with everything sort of tone a sapping of their courage to continue it.

Though your service ought to have created something of a right atmosphere for your sermon, it is well to start your sermon also on a middle key, always bearing in mind that you cannot assume, but must create, the interest in your subject which your own previous concentration on it has given you.

Bear in mind also, especially if you are affirming anything worth standing for, that you may have prejudices as well as preoccupations to dispel. The difficulty is that merely to mention them may only make people realise that they cherish them, whereupon every reason you urge against them becomes a reason for holding them more tenaciously. Therefore the great art is to remove them without stirring them up by frontal attack.

A great master of this art was the Apostle Paul. Take for example the Colossian heresy. Whatever may be thought of the letters to Timothy, such sayings as 'fables and endless genealogies,' 'profane and old wives' tales,' 'foolish and ignorant questions,' look like the Apostle's private opinion about it, for it is improbable that anyone else had a mind so free and independent as to think so courageously. In the Colossian Epistle, as he finds that it is being taken seriously, he has to treat it with more respect, yet that it was a very select, esoteric, high-browed mystery sort of article, we gather only from what the Apostle sets up against it. As it had been expounded too much already, he just states the opposite truth and leaves it to correct error. Before his readers knew what he was after, he begins by ringing the changes on the word *all*, to affirm that the glory of Christianity is its comprehensiveness of all men and its condescension to all things, and then simply exalts the spiritual significance of the common life and common humanity, in contrast to the vanity of being made superior persons by a philosophy which knew the secrets of the heavens and an asceticism to deliver from the desires of earth.

Having begun aright, the next task is to proceed aright. For this there is one broad rule. Move forward from the intellect to the heart and conscience.

You begin with the intellect partly because, if you start on a high emotional key, you will have great difficulty in keeping it up, and more in advancing on it, but mainly because, if it is not plain what you are saying and why you are saying it, the result will not be genuine feeling, but only a kind of contagion of rhetorical fervour, which can degenerate into an almost physical stimulus, pernicious even if only evanescent. As we have seen, a true and helpful and enlightened conviction is different from a merely sentimental or sensational impression precisely because it has an intellectual basis. Moreover few minds can afford to do without a logical order, even if only made to be left behind. A disciplined army may break up in assault, but even then it is very different from an undisciplined rabble.

The succour of a logical arrangement, however, is not confined to this intellectual basis.

The venerable questions—The What ? The Why ? And the Whereto ? embody it, if not quite so simply as the negro preacher's method : " First I explains the tex, then I presents the argyments, then I puts in the rousements."

The presentation of the truth you would enforce may neither be by expounding your text, nor by any statement of a principle. In one way or another, however, you must make plain to your hearers what it is

all about, before you either ask them to believe it or to
act upon it, or even to proceed with you at all in considering it. The working up of a desperate state of confused
earnestness only makes people wonder what the pother
is about. Urgent appeals for belief in what is still in
the clouds and for immediate and self-denying action
for no one knows what is mere beating the air, though
the whole meaning of your message should be growing
clearer by all you say.

Again, though you should convince the mind before
you have any right to appeal to the heart, it is not necessarily by argument or reasoning at all. There are evils to
assail and sophisms to expose, but mere argument seldom
does either. " Come now and let us reason together "
does not mean come and let us have a bout of discussion
to see who wins, but come and lay our minds alongside of
each other that we may help each other to see the truth.
All other reasoning is mere logomachy. And as it is
the truth itself which alone has a right to convince, the
most convincing reasoning against error is just to present
the highest truth you see as you see it and as it appeals
to you. You must not merely ask for belief, but must
make it believable by showing it to be true which you
do best by presenting truth in its own persuasiveness
and leaving it to do the convincing. Similarly you
can only effectively overcome evil with good. The
greatest example is the Master Himself. One might
almost say He never argues. When the Sadducees
would argue about the resurrection, He merely states
the great incontrovertible faith that " God is not the
God of the dead but of the living." And though He
exposed evil, it was by showing the disaster of rejecting
the counsel of God. Whereby every word He ever
uttered is persuasive, and remains persuasive to this
day.

The final effect of your preaching should be before
you from the start, and every word you utter should be
directed towards it, and not merely be one of the heads
of your discourse ; and still less a word of exhortation

at the end. No discourse is really edifying unless all of it is concerned with stirring the heart and touching the conscience and moving the will, and the final word should be to clench the nail which the whole has been fastening in a sure place, and not a closing tap which if it do anything will only help to drive it out.

This end is not necessarily to do something. Higher and better is to be something. And for this the greatest may be an inspiring, stimulating, helpful belief, above all a deeper faith in God through Jesus Christ, and the assurance that all life's common tasks and common relationships are blessed and succoured by peace with Him of Whom are all things.

This may be endeavoured in either of two ways. One is to show how the highest and sublimest religious truths touch life in its humblest duties and simplest needs ; the other is to show that the commonest experiences have in them the burden of the most sublime truths and most exalted duties. The most used way is the former, and we have a supreme example of it in the Sermon on the Mount, where the highest principles of the righteousness of the kingdom of heaven are brought down to the very practical everyday dangers upon earth of anger, impurity, falsehood, revenge, hypocrisy, covetousness, censoriousness. Our Lord does not denounce these sins. He sets them over against the blessedness of the true righteousness, as the squandering of our divine heritage : and in the end He leaves men with God and not with their own good resolution.

Yet the other is His more favourite form of teaching. He met all kinds of common incidents, incidents which to others would have been merely trivial or even irritating, and He was asked all kinds of shallow and sometimes not very sincere questions, and He lifted them up to the kingdom of God by such parables as The Prodigal Son and The Good Samaritan and The Lost Sheep, or He showed, even from foolish rivalry, the spirit of God's rule and His care for all His children. And what is even the Lord's Supper but the passing from the commonest uses of the material to the sublimest heights of the spiritual ?

There is hardly any practical question that cannot be thus exalted, and, what is more, there is no other right answer to it. Suppose, for example, you feel called to speak of gambling. For it there are no end of subtle defences, and if you confine yourself to rebutting them you will not get far. But how does gambling look to a man with the sense that he has nothing he has not received, and that this is only blessed as it is talent committed to his care by God for His service ? And there are few if any common evils to which the true answer is anything less than the whole mind of God in Jesus Christ, and no duties that are really virtues apart from one's whole faith as well as one's whole life.

XX

PLAN

(a) DIVISIONS

THE first requirement is to see your subject in some
kind of clear perspective. This needs unity of plan :
and for it divisions, within limits, may be at least
helpful if they are on one principle and to one end.

The most elaborate use of the method of dividing
and sub-dividing I have ever come across was by a
German professor. He had such an elaborate system
of Gross A, Klein A, Römisch Eins, Arabisches Eins,
that he sometimes got bogged in them himself and the
students had to pull him out of the quagmire. But
preaching in Scotland was at one time so much of this
type that young people were often provided with note-
books in which to put down what were known as
'heads and remarks.' No doubt it was an admirable
way of keeping them awake, but probably not by being
interested.

Many of the greatest preachers have used no other
form of division than the pause. And it may be argued
that divisions, especially if announced, however much
they may aid unity of plan, hinder progressive impression, which for some subjects and some forms of impression is certainly true. You are therefore not to
be enslaved to divisions or any method, but use what
best serves your purpose : and probably, as your
mastery increases, the value of at least set divisions may
decrease.

Yet the custom of using divisions in preaching having developed widely and independently and been
used by the greatest preachers, who could not be

o

suspected of being driven to the practice from lack of ability to find a better way, it must have some good reason. And if it was helpful to them, probably it will be more so to you, especially at the beginning of your ways.

You have both to interrupt and to sustain your discourse. You have not to hurry your hearers on in one breathless rush, but to give them resting-places, from which they can look back over the way they have passed and be encouraged by glimpses of what is to come. Above all, when you rise to greater heights, you must come down again to the common level.

For these ends, not only clear points, but definite announced divisions, may be the succour you need. This may not be the best of all possible ways, but it does enable you to finish one particular aspect of the subject and to begin the next on the level of ordinary conversational speech, which at all events is better than keeping up at a level where your oratory degenerates into wordy rhetoric, or flounders through a quagmire of ' nows ' and ' buts,' or is lost in a debatable land of pomposity and platitude. Even for merely passing from one point to another, you may find heads as stepping-stones better at least than taking a flying leap, which leaves your audience wondering what possible connection there may be.

Yet it should never be more than a help. You may not merely say : Now we have done with that point, let us proceed to the next. You have to sustain as well as interrupt your discourse, and even divisions should be so handled as to make the transition from one point to another not only simple and natural, but of obvious sequence. For this they must be the true divisions of the one subject, and not a mere device for having another subject or two to flee to, if you fail to evoke the liberality of the first. More especially you may need their aid in the matter of proportion, because it is easy to beat out what should be only preliminary, and then have no time to do justice to the vital issue.

Helpful divisions must be on one progressive principle and to one end, and be like articulated joints, which have still the coherence of what is united, with the freedom of what is separate. As an example you can look at F. W. Robertson's sermons. His divisions even by themselves are the natural, sequent divisions of the subject, as clearly one as they are definitely distinct.

If you can come by such divisions, they will also be a gain to the hearer, whom and not himself the preacher should be out to profit. Except perhaps a very striking illustration, few things are more memorable than a pithy, proportionate, progressive division, and it helps also to make memorable all the rest.

Given the right divisions, we may thus sum up their benefits. They help the preacher to clarify and develop his thought, to proceed easily from one part to another, and to secure a right proportion of the whole; and they give the hearer pegs on which to hang what he hears, and resting-places and points of outlook by the way.

If divisions are to fulfil this purpose, they must be real, one might say inevitable divisions of the one subject, and a genuine aid both to working it out and to carrying it home; while helping to clearness they must neither interrupt the impression nor destroy the shading; and they must themselves be memorable and an aid to memory.

Brevity is the soul of the titles of divisions, as it is of wit. A long rambling summary neither develops the subject nor helps the hearer, but only dismays.

Concreteness is equally important. The more abstract they are, the less they help you to work out your subject and the less they aid the hearer. A division for example of " If any man will come after me, let him deny himself and take up his cross and follow me " into the Christian Principle—Let a man deny himself; the Christian Practice—Take up his cross; the Christian Pattern—Follow Me, though in a sense adequate, is nevertheless likely to prove merely three large unmanageable abstractions.

Again, divisions should be memorable.

The division just given raises the question of alliteration as an aid. It is dangerous, and *p* is a specially dangerous letter, though *q* runs it hard. The result is apt to be what an address which had two heads with *p's* and two with *q's* was called, ' a very peculiar speech.' But while it is a fond thing to search for alliteration, there is no reason for rejecting it if it arrive for a better reason than mere ingenuity. Like endings to lines are used by modern poetry to make it memorable, but like beginnings once served the same purpose, as in the line ' Lightly down leaping he loosened his harness.' Other things being equal, therefore, if your division is thus made more memorable, take it as a gift.

Finally divisions should be few. When the parson comes to Fifthly, he should stop for a better reason than being perplexed. Not only are many divisions unprofitable, but the natural divisions are seldom more than twofold or threefold. Certain minds tend to two and others to three, but it is better to realise that they serve different purposes. Two usually opens up a subject better, and may be most helpful when your main business is to expound a truth, but three may bring it better together to enforce a practical end.

In a sense they may be determined by the old questions, the What ? the Why ? and the Whereto ? but only in a very vague sense, if you are to have a treatment varied according to the quality of your subject and the needs of your hearers. You will not long have very attentive hearers, and for the good reason that your treatment will be as shallow as it is stale, should your habitual method be to say, *firstly*, this is the truth I mean to impress upon you ; *secondly*, this is why I think it worth impressing ; *thirdly*, now I am going to insist upon it. The end to be gained should be before you from the beginning, the truth to be presented should shine clear from first to last, and the ground for believing and acting on it should be growing clearer in the whole presentation.

The sole test not only of divisions, but of all methods of treatment, is that it really manifests the truth in its graciousness, its sublimity and power. If divisions help to this end they are good, if not then not. Yet divisions of some kind will be helpful to you at the beginning, though probably you will and possibly you should become more independent of their aid as you acquire greater freedom with your subject and more experience in the ways of reaching the minds of your hearers.

Even then however you will likely have divisions though you do not announce them: and the only question remaining is, whether if you do announce them, you should announce them all at once, or only when you come to each one in your progress. This plainly depends on your purpose. If it is mainly teaching, it is a gain to be able to repeat your points; if it is mainly practical, it may not be wise at once to show your hand, for, as it has been expressed, a sermon should not only have a plan but also a plot.

(b) INTRODUCTION

It might seem that, as the introduction is the beginning, it ought to have been considered first. But the chief use of divisions is to mark out the ground before beginning to build. The introduction is the porch by which you enter, but its character should be determined by what the whole is to be.

So much is this the case that you may even have received the advice to prepare your introduction, as you might a preface, only when the rest is completed. But the result is likely to be, like many porches, obviously stuck on. Though last in conception, if it is to be a true introduction, it must be first in execution. The reason why it is both difficult and important is that it cannot be right till you have the whole in your mind's eye, and so is the kind of beginning which is well begun half done.

This relation to the whole undertaking, makes it second in difficulty only to the conclusion. It will start so far away from your subject that it helps you in no way to reach it; or so near that you find yourself plunged into the middle at the start. It will be so large and abstract as to lead you away from anything that concerns the actual life of your hearers; or so practical and concrete that you are at the application before you have presented any truth to apply. It will be so lively that you cannot keep it up, much less advance on it; or so dull and ponderous as to be merely the administration of a soporific, the effect of which may last throughout the whole discourse. You try a textual introduction, and you annex your first head; or a contextual, and it becomes a commentary on the whole book. You start from some general theme, with the result that you might have it stereotyped as permanent introduction to any possible subject.

In your bad days the task will bring you to the verge of despair. Yet it is precisely in your worst days that persistence is most profitable. The only thing to do is to tear up and start afresh, not once or twice only, but till you arrive. Even then you cannot promise yourselves a glowing success. A measure of it, however, can hardly fail if you endure hardness till the battle is won, because you cannot win till you see the end from the beginning, without which good work cannot be done. As this may be a weary struggle, you may be tempted to abandon it in despair. But to surrender to difficulties is a weakness and to form a habit of it a disaster. Nor is it only that mountaineers are made by facing up to steep places. The steep beginning also leads most quickly to the widest prospect. So your hindrances may prove your helps if you go on till you do start right. Even then you had better eschew personal explanation as an intro-duction, and more particularly the kind which raises expectations. Buffalo Bill's prescription for success, "Advertise well, and come up to your advertisement" may be true for shows, but preaching should not be a show.

About the introduction there are just two rules. The first is that it must really introduce; and the second is like unto it, it must only introduce.

The second I take first, because it is mainly concerned with the danger already mentioned, of the introduction overshadowing the discourse. An introduction is to create interest, not to satisfy it. It should be only one point, and not too much of it. Above all it must avoid what an old woman said about John Owen, that he was so long spreading the table that she lost her appetite for the meal. But on this I say no more, not because the error is rare or of little consequence or easy to avoid, but for the reason that, beyond warning, there is no more to be said.

The first point, however, of an introduction which really introduces, is much more complex. While it is better to have no introduction than one which oversteps its business, it is seldom that you have a subject into the middle of which you can plunge with profit. And even if your subject need no introduction, your audience does. If for nothing else, they need a little time to settle down. But also they start the better for being first drawn both towards you and your subject, and they will travel with you more hopefully if they can survey the scene for a little before taking the road.

Your attitude towards your audience should be a little like Cook's guide at Chamonix, a German Swiss, whom I knew only by the name of Franz. As we were starting one morning about five o'clock for the Mer de Glace, he explained his procedure. "I gather them all together. They have not risen perhaps in their lives at this hour before. They have not taken breakfast very comfortable, and are still half asleep. We start ver slow, and I must put them in a good humour. The ladies come to me and say, 'Is it ver far?' And I say, 'O no madam, it is no distance at all,' unless it is a French woman with high-heeled shoes and a long train. Then I say, 'O madam, it is a ver long distance,' and she turn. A guide who cannot tell a little lie to encourage his people at the start is no guide at all. But then I go faster and faster." This at least was true, as I found when he left me with two strange ladies, who had utterly lost their heads on the Mauvais Pas, and whom I had to take down, one on each arm, with their eyes shut.

From this you may learn not to go faster at any point than your audience can travel with you. But the advice to start slow and with the kind of introduction which gathers them all together and enables them to step out with you is worth taking. And while it may not be a little lie, it might be a little fable, if this does the main business of starting them in good heart.

It is not enough, therefore, to ask what kind of introduction your subject needs. It may be even more necessary to ask what kind your audience needs. So far as your subject is concerned, it might be enough to explain the context, but so far as your audience is concerned, this may be mere dissipation of interest. Even if you judge this to be the right beginning, you must confine yourself to what your hearers actually require, and make this interesting to them and not merely a display of your own erudition.

Your subject may also need introduction, but it will suffice to sum up generally the purposes an introduction may serve.

(1) If you have a subject which might raise difficulties or stir prejudices, it is a great art to be able to dispose of them at the start without ever seeming to bring them forward. But you must take care that you are not merely bringing them forward without disposing of them, so that all you do is to give them a long run from start to finish.

(2) To heighten the effect of what you have to say by contrast or to explain away what might seem to be in

conflict with some other truth. Yet you must beware
of sending the minds of your hearers off on the opposite
track or of leaving on them the impression that what
you say is at best half a truth.

(3) To connect your subject with larger principles and
show that it is no isolated question either in Scripture
or life. Only you must not bury the interest of your
subject even in the greater issues, nor launch out into
the infinite.

(4) To refresh the commonplace. Though this would
be the best of all introductions, if you could attain it, it
must make your hearers discover something vital and
profound which they have long looked at but never
really seen before, and not be a mere tarnishing still
further by dull repetition. Also it must be really there
to be shown and not something merely dragged in.

(c) CONCLUSION

This is even more difficult than the introduction.

As the introduction should be like the porch, first in
execution but last in conception, the conclusion should
be like the spire, last in execution but first in conception.
As you have to prepare for the spire by laying foundation
strong enough to bear it, and erect thereon pillars,
buttressed by the whole building, able to support it, so
every word you say should not only be leading up to the
conclusion, but have throughout power to sustain it.
Though preaching is more than mere pleading, there is
a sense in which, like a barrister addressing a jury, you
should be out, from beginning to end, for a verdict.
And the conclusion should only be, like his, the most
impressive, most telling appeal to clench all that has been
already said.

An easy but ineffectual way is to conclude by what
might always be prefaced by : " Now my dear brethren
for a few words of exhortation and practical application."
Even with this rather simple warning that relief is
nigh, it might still be effective did it indicate the

concentration of the wrestler who waits to spring for his last grip at his adversary. But if, for example, it is a pause to take off the spectacles and wipe them and replace them carefully, it is an act of turning aside which dissipates every impression and destroys every hope that it will ever be carried home to any vital purpose.

Yet there are even worse ways than this of ending, or rather of being unable to end. It is not merely that many otherwise good sermons are spoiled by weak, inconclusive conclusions, but there are people, in public as in private speech, who seem to have a constitutional unwillingness to wind up at all. " He's done and we're all done, but he can't stop," might be harsh judgment, but the more genial criticism, " He came past several good stopping-places," is too often amply justified. Such conclusions might be arranged in the form with which Professor Blackie, who was supposed to be professor of Greek but freely indulged himself in being professor of things in general, used to allow himself scope. Partly in caricature and partly in humorous awareness of his own weakness, he slowed down to a close, with " In the pre-pro-penultimate place," and after he arrived at the ultimate place, had still " Finally and in a word," which word was by no means in the singular.

This raises the question of how far the last word should be distant from the first. The answer should depend both on the subject you have to expound and on the impression you wish to make. Subjects are not necessarily made clear in proportion to the number of words you employ, nor the impression according to the time taken in attempting to make it, yet nothing is worth discussing which does not take some time to explain nor any impression worth trying to make which can be flung off in a sentence or two. Just here, however, is the trouble. A difficult subject is precisely what people cannot attend to long, and one with which they do not agree what they will not endure beyond narrow limits.

The actual length of time you may take depends therefore on the interest you can sustain. Given a subject deserving of interest and a way of treating it that makes it interesting, the limits are liberal. Here speaking goes a long way and picturesqueness of presentation goes still farther. If you have the gift of easy, natural, varied, moving speech and have been granted a voice that carries music to the ear as well as meaning to the mind, and you can be graphic and vivid, you need not keep your eye too anxiously on the clock. The longest sermon I ever heard, well over an hour, seemed the shortest, because it was delivered as a kind of chant by perhaps the most flexible and melodious voice I ever heard, and was lit up by a fancy which made the hearer see visions and dream dreams. On the other hand, two ten-minutes' discourses were of a tedium that was like ten minutes on the rack, because there was neither substance, nor form, nor tolerable delivery.

In this as in all else you must preserve your liberty. If you are finished in twenty minutes, then stop, however well you are maintaining attention, but, if not, go on as long as you can sustain attention. Only be sure that you have the gift for sustaining it, not only by the painful effort of your hearers, but by their happy absorption in interest, before you venture to encroach upon the second half-hour. A serious subject may need the first half-hour if it is to be treated adequately, but you will be well advised, till you have proved your gifts, and even after that, unless they are very exceptional, not greatly to trespass on the second.

Like the master of assemblies, your words should be the words of the wise, and should end when wisdom ends. It is not enough just to stop, for even the words of wisdom are to be as nails fastened in a sure place, and your last word should be the right word so to fasten them.

XXI

ILLUSTRATION

ILLUSTRATION is not a subject by itself, but merely part of the whole task of presenting thought concretely as well as clearly, and good only as it is one with the thought and the best way of presenting it. The treatment of it in isolation might suggest that you make a collection of illustrations and then, at certain points of your discourse, say to yourselves, this needs an illustration, and proceed to select from your store the least inappropriate. And no doubt this can be done. But the result would probably be the diverting of your thought to the display of your illustration, rather than the subordination of your illustration to the illumination of your thinking. Wherefore there is only the usual justification for considering the subject by itself, that the human mind, by reason of its limitation, has to distinguish where it ought not to divide.

Nowhere is the value of illustrations and the need to give thought to them more evident than in the most perfect example, our Lord's parables. They are not appended to His teaching, but are the effective vehicle through which He taught, and it is impossible to believe that the conveying of His message through picture and in intimate relation to the world of nature and of men was not a considered method to which He had given much thought. For us at least not the vaguest approach to such perfection could be possible without much study.

Though this might be sufficient justification for special consideration of the subject, for students there is the still further reason, that the student's life is but

220

ILLUSTRATION 221

poor training for the mastery of this art of embodying thought in picture.

Conversation, reading and writing should all be fruitful fields for illustrations, but while the student has in this respect a larger field than others, he is at a disadvantage in cultivating it. His conversation with people is apt to turn towards large and general questions ; much of his reading is concerned with absorbing the main ideas and impressions of his author ; his writing is mostly summaries for his own use or condensed indications of his knowledge for teachers or examiners who know the subject better than himself.

The first and most difficult task is to realise the new situation when you come to speak to people who are not bound to give you their attention, but whose interest must both be arrested and sustained, and who may be as able to think as you can when the truth is incarnated in life, but cannot cope with disembodied abstractions.

To the end no doubt there will be among you great differences in fertility. Yet if you realise this necessity of bringing, as it were, things and thought together, you will none of you find yourselves wholly lacking in the gift of discovering the illustrations which present your thought in picture and not in mere naked idea. The wrong kind of teacher in the pulpit is one who pins his faith to mere repetition and rubbing it in, forgetting that he has not the teacher's power to insist on his hearers bending their mind to the effort. What tells is the winged word that shoots home and sticks : and this may be by an unforgettable illustration.

The difficulty is that you cannot acquire your thought in this form. A student who reads a stiff book and notes only the rare illustrations, may prove a popular and even a profitable preacher for two years, but the third shows that he has no vision of truth down the long vistas of which people may look and see more and more beyond. To be able to go on for a lifetime, you must have much knowledge acquired in condensed and even abstract form and do a great deal of the same kind of thinking for yourself. Yet a great preacher would be like a great poet, one who has faced abstract questions so thoroughly and in such intimate bearing on the world and men, that they have become incarnate for him in nature and human nature and life's many forms and changes. Possibly we never really know any truth till we thus see it incarnated.

Illustration in the form of simile is only one part, and perhaps the smaller part. The other is metaphor, or akin to metaphor—not merely the illuminating and enforcing of the thought by a picture, but the embodying of it in the image. To the Hebrew who had seen so much disaster descend upon his nation through a defile which he called the Valley of Achor or Troubling, " I have set the Valley of Achor for a door of hope," needed no elaboration of it as an illustration of the general statement that good may come out of evil. But even where there is ' as ' or ' like ' or such words of comparison, the image may still incarnate the thought and not merely illustrate it. " Behold I send you forth as sheep in the midst of wolves," is a simile in form, but it is a metaphor in effect. " The kingdom of heaven is like unto " is a simile in form, yet the thought is not given and the mustard seed and the leaven added to explain it, but the figure is the thought itself. Shakespeare is supreme in metaphor, but even his similes generally have the thought so embedded in the figure as to be one with it.

> Like as the waves make towards the pebbled shore,
> So do our minutes hasten to their end,
> Each changing place with that which goes before,
> In sequent toil all forwards do contend.

In form this is a simile, an illustration, but in fact there is no other expression of the thought than the figure, and perhaps no human words ever brought home the fleeting quality of the most general of all human experiences, which is time, or fixed it more in a simple fact of nature—the sequent forward toil of the waves ending

ILLUSTRATION 223

on the beach. On the other hand, we have the statement of the general principle :

> O no; the apprehension of the good
> Gives but the greater feeling to the worse :

and while there is no indication of simile, what goes
before is just illustration.

> O who can hold a fire in his hand,
> By thinking of the frosty Caucasus ?
> Or cloy the hungry edge of appetite,
> By bare imagination of a feast ?
> Or wallow naked in December snow,
> By thinking on fantastic summer heat ?

Illustration by quotations must be good in themselves and apt to the connection before they are of profit,
and be specially clearly spoken if they are to be followed.
As even Homer nods, the greatest name does not
guarantee the greatness of an utterance : and even the
highest wisdom most nobly expressed may still be
irrelevant to your immediate purpose. An almost
unconscious freedom of allusion is more valuable than
a conscious selecting of quotations, though there may be
times when a quotation has so come home to your heart
and so perfectly expresses what you would say that it
may be incomparably weightier than any words of your
own. And if you never fall into the habit of mere repetition without having it called forth by living experience
of their truth, this is specially true of quotations from
Scripture. Quote anything you like when it thus stirs
you. Yet excessive quotatiousness is almost as dangerous a gift as excessive loquaciousness.

The first purpose of an illustration is just to illustrate,
to make truth simpler and clearer. To this end it should
be used only for what is difficult to the hearer. This
may seem so obvious as to be unnecessary to mention ;
but it is not altogether rare to hear what is simple and
even trivial brought on with a whole bevy of attendant
illustrations, and what alone is both difficult and important shot off in one sweeping general statement. Further,

it should be an illustration which illustrates. This also requires to be said, because sometimes the illustration has more need of explanation than the truth it is supposed to explain. Most illustrations from science and not a few from history are of this character, such as Relativity or the Epicureans and Stoics.

The second, after making a truth easier to understand, would be to make it easier to appreciate and remember. For the former purpose very familiar illustrations might be useful, and perhaps the more unfamiliar the truth the more familiar may be the illustration, but for this purpose of arousing and sustaining interest, freshness is needed as well as picturesqueness. Unfortunately the better, more original and more effective your illustration, the less you can use it again for the same audience. It may even be the only thing remembered. But you would not wish to be able to use what you have said over and over again because you are comfortably assured that no one will ever recall it.

If we name the first purpose enlightenment and the second appreciation, the third is persuasion.

While the advice to 'shun metaphor in argument like the devil' is sound, misrepresentation or prejudice, or even unreason, may be met by illustration more effectively than by any argument.

In the days when Fair Trade was the slogan and the most conflicting promises were being made to various sectional interests, a very old friend carried an election by this illustration. "It is like a man who lived in a village outside of Paris during the Revolution, who meeting a friend fresh from the city asked what was happening. 'It is awful,' was the reply, 'they are cutting off heads by the thousand.' 'Good heavens!' he cried, 'surely not heads. Why, I'm a hatter.'" Even as argument, this would take a lot of solemn reasoning to beat. Nay, solemn argument may be the last way of meeting many situations. How much vehement argument and denunciation would have been needed against frivolous ecclesiastical cursing to have

ILLUSTRATION   225

been as effective as Knox's one good-humoured illustration, " Ane auld wife has tint a spurtle (*i.e.* a porridge-stick). God's curse and mine on him who kens o' this gear and does not restore it."

The greatest example of dealing with a wrong attitude by way of illustration is the Parable of the Good Samaritan. It is not reasoning according to the canons of Formal Logic, but if the end of reasoning is to bring minds into conformity with truth, not propositions into conformity with rules, it does the business.

Persuasion, however, has to do with more than changing an opinion or even a way of looking at things. Perhaps oratory, in the accepted sense, is only possible when the orator and his audience have common ground in their general outlook. His business is less to alter conviction than to make people feel more deeply what is involved and to persuade them to act upon it. For this purpose even a well-worn illustration, if effectively presented, may be more profitable because of its familiarity. Possibly the orator generally is rather fertile and felicitous than original in the use of illustration. Persuading men to action may even be better done by rallying what is accepted to his aid, than by sending their minds off in new channels. If presented vividly and to practical purpose for a great truth or a worthy end, people may almost be persuaded that an illustration is new, though quite aware that it is as well-worn as the old half-sovereign in the days when it was current coin.

The most persuasive illustrations, however, deal both with experiences which belong to all men, and present them in forms that are original. The greatest example is the Parable of the Prodigal Son. Though there is not a person or an incident in it we could not most of us parallel, what depths both in man's heart and God's it searches, just as a story and not by morals attached to it, and how fresh it is every time it is read !

This raises the question of the story as illustration. If it is an anecdote with a moral stuck on to it or at

P

best sticking out of it, it will probably not go far to prove that 'Truth embodied in a tale may enter in at lowly doors.' For this it must be embodied in the tale itself, not following it like a pale ghost. So to be able to tell a story is a talent few possess. Many who believe they have it are only too apt to degenerate into what has been called their 'anecdotage,' but when truly possessed, it is a great gift.

Let the stories be frankly fiction by all means, as the story of the Prodigal Son is, shocking as it may appear to some good realistic people, who would be comforted to know that it had all taken place exactly as related. But strange as it may seem in these days of the out-pouring of the secrets of the life and of the soul, our Lord never produces one of His own experiences, He invents His stories, often not much within the range of His own experience, as about rich men and kings.

Just because you have not this power, you may have to fall back on actual happenings you have seen or heard of. And so long as you do not make yourself the hero round which it all turns, this may be to the good. But relating stories in the first person is to some people a sort of necessary literary embellishment. It is dangerous in all cases, and when the stories are obviously dressed up, not for the purpose of making them better illustrations but for the glorification of the narrator, it may give the impression not any longer of what is frankly fiction, but of what is ostentatiously lies. Tall personal experiences are sometimes given, especially in evangelistic addresses, which challenge the credulity because, while truth may be stranger than fiction, its improbabilities are of rarer occurrence.

You may still suffer from the poverty which cannot provide better. But all that illustration should do, and what is good taste in using it, will be plain if you regard the real business of illustration as only a part of the one fact that good preaching, while it passes by the external trappings of life to realise the worth of the soul and deal with its essential needs, never forgets that

ILLUSTRATION 227

man not only lives in the world and amid the common doings of men, but has to fulfil God's purpose by them, even if it be by denying them. Make men feel that, though you are first and last concerned with their spiritual needs, their immortal lives, their eternal interests, you never forget how these must be cared for amid life's manifold temptations, its daily drudgery, its varied trials, its mixed human relations, its vanities and its humiliations, and though you may never be great preachers, you will not fail to console and encourage, to warn and to challenge, and in short to get the best kind of hearing, perhaps the only kind worth having. It comes back to this, that you go about the world with the sense that in every human soul you may meet the Master Himself, and that you meet people as He did, in God's common transitory world, which yet has in it His spiritual and eternal purpose.

XXII

THE MINISTRY OF THE WORD

THE old name, "The Ministry of the Word," includes not only your preaching but all your work, if you understand by the Word of God what even the Scriptures only serve. Yet there is no inspiration for it and no help for maintaining it like searching the Scriptures and right use of them. With it, all your other reading will be profitable to this end; without it, all your other reading will not suffice. As the father said to his son about honesty being the best policy, " I know, for I have tried both ways." If not merely with your ear hearing it, but with your eye seeing it, you discover how much the Bible is the most wonderful book in the world, it will afford you endlessly varied inspiration and endlessly full instruction.

Though it should never be to you a mere compendium of texts, you need it for texts, and it does provide them with unparalleled variety of inspiration and enlightenment, if only you have insight to discover them for yourselves.

About the use of a text there is no universal rule more than about anything else, except its profit : and if you can do better without, by all means exercise your freedom. Yet, even if only as a motto, the use of a text is usually of profit. There are few truths worth preaching about for which you cannot find a motto in Scripture which will so far represent your subject as to buttress it by what is still a little weightier authority than your own, and show at least that it is no mere personal idiosyncracy.

These ends, however, will not be served by forcing meaning on the words or selecting phrases torn from their contexts.

228

Probably you know the story about Bishop Wilber-
force and the curate. " What have you been preaching
on ? " " On ' Hear the Church.' " " But there is no
such text in the Bible." " Surely, my lord, ' If any man
will not hear the Church.' " " Well, I will give you
another for next Sunday. ' Hang all the law and the
prophets.' "

You may be more plausible than this, and yet be
even more apart from the real meaning. For example,
" Until the day dawn and the shadows flee away," has
been used more than once as a motto on tombstones and
as a text for funeral sermons. But though there may
be more in the idea of the Song of Solomon as a spiritual
allegory than people ignorant of the oriental mind may
conceive possible, if you read the whole verse, " Let us
take our fill of loves till the day dawn and the shadows
flee away," you could not readily bring yourselves to
think that this particular verse of it was ever intended
for either purpose.

Exercise your liberty by all means, so long as it is
not quite this kind of licence, and have subjects and
use texts only as mottos or have no text at all. Yet,
as a general habit, preaching on a text and not merely
with one, and that in its exact meaning, is a great safe-
guard for keeping out of ruts both in matter and
treatment.

Why should you not simply announce that you propose
to preach on the virtue of meekness, or the doctrine of
the forgiveness of sins, or on the love of God ? You
may, of course, but the danger is that, starting with a
large colourless abstraction in the void, you will never
bring it down to any actual interest of man's daily life or
appeal by it to any prevailing mood of the human soul.
You will not be saved merely by taking a text if, as is
a common habit of students, you treat it as crude ore,
and put it in the alembic of your minds to extract from
it a general idea, or, what is worse, two or three, and
throw away the rest as alloy. As what is most valuable
is truth, not in the abstract but in life and action, you

thereby lose what is of most profit.   The greatest source
of variety is to work your way not into the truth alone,
but into the mood, the temper, the attitude towards
life, the special angle of vision, the particular practical
bearing of your text.   This may be summed up as variety
of approach.

Take for example the subjects already mentioned.

Are you likely to make much more of the mere general
doctrine of meekness than a rather feeble passivity?
But if you work your way into the mind of Jesus when
He said, "The meek shall inherit the earth," you will
at once realise that it is no passivity, but the active
acceptance of God's will, active for men's trials as well
as for their tasks, and is the mightiest power both for
meeting all life's ills and for possessing all life's abiding
blessings, because it is the only emancipation from fear,
which, however violently it may fight for its own hands,
is weakness and inherits nothing.

The forgiveness of sins you should often preach on :
but when you have discussed and enforced it merely as
a doctrine, you have shot your bolt, and any return to
it will be mere reiteration.   Besides, you may leave the
impression that it has only to do with another life, and
only with a God far away in the heavens, and an arrangement for meeting Him on easier terms some day, and
that, even so, it is a lot of fuss about what are at worst
peccadilloes, and anyhow are over and done with.   But
the relations of forgiveness to God and man and life
in Scripture are endless, and because of those intimate
personal settings, never leave on the mind the impression
that the corruption of the human heart is merely a
theological phrase about total depravity, or sins mere
breaking laws and forgiveness of them mere condoning
consequences, all conceived in the atmosphere of the
law courts.   Sin has many aspects, and none of them
merely sins.   If you enable men's eyes, like Isaiah's, to
see the King the Lord of Hosts, they will know that they
have unclean lips which need to be purged ; if you set
before them the blessed fulness of His rule, they will

know why Paul cries out, "O wretched man that I am"; if you show them the Father who is kind to the unthankful and evil, they will know that sin is against their own souls; if you show them the mind of Christ, they will never again make light of sinning against others. Above all, if you teach as He taught and lived, you will show that forgiveness is concerned with God's love and active mercy, and not with judgment and wrath. This has to do with the cross, but as the highest evidence, in face of all human wickedness, that the mercy of God is infinite, and that nothing His wisdom and goodness can accomplish will be spared. In short it is the perfect way of beseeching men to be reconciled, and not His sole and exclusive way of giving pardon and peace.

On the love of God I am not sure that you should ever preach generally. A good and thoughtful and devout man said, "I am tired of hearing in sermons about love. After all it is only said once in the Bible that God is love." What he was weary of was not the reality, which was the centre of all his faith, but the unreality of mere sentimental repetition till the very word became nauseous. Like the Apostle's great lyric on it, you must make it into a grand sweet song before it will sing its way into men's hearts, and then enable them to see in all common experience, however partially and dimly, that God's love knows them and directs their way, however imperfectly they know it. When our Lord makes God's kindness to the unthankful and evil His supreme perfection, which we are to seek in loving them that hate us and praying for those who use us despitefully, there is no danger of ending in vapid, unreal, unpractical sentiment.

Again let us take two texts about perfection and see with what variety the Bible enables you to treat a subject which by itself can be the narrowest observance of negative rules and the ground of a self-satisfaction which is the end of forgetting the things that are behind and reaching forward to those that are before, and to show that neither time nor eternity can ever exhaust it.

The first is the text already quoted, " Be ye perfect as your heavenly Father is perfect," Matt. v. 48. The other is, " That we present every man perfect in Christ Jesus," Col. i. 28. The mere subject is the same in both, and as one has to do with God and the other with Christ, it cannot be thought of as any kind of finality. But consider how different are the thoughts, the situations, the audiences, the misunderstandings, the motives to which appeal is made. Jesus finds men tried more than they can bear by slander and ill usage ; the Apostle finds them puffed up by exalted notions and ascetic morality. Jesus sets men in the midst of God's gracious rule in an evil world, to deal with its evil as He does, in the assurance that this is the only adequate way of overcoming it. Paul sets them in the fellowship of which Christ is pattern and power, and appeals to each member's responsibility for the progress of others. Not only have you intimate relations to different aspects of experience, which makes them quite different subjects, but if you realise these relations, you can neither descend to mere negative ideas of perfection, nor turn its positive requirement into moral platitude.

Here is the value of incidents. They give not to ' airy nothings,' but to great doctrines of faith, and principles of practice, which need them even more, ' a local habitation and a name.'

Take the wise woman of Tekoah, 2 Sam. xiv. 14, " For we must needs die and are as water spilt on the ground, which cannot be gathered up again, yet he will not destroy, but doth devise means that his banished be not expelled from him." She pleads that mercy is an attribute of God Himself, active mercy, wise in devising effective means ; and she also brings it home to mortal man, by setting it in the midst of our common frailty and evanescence. Catch this mood as it melts and glows, and then say what you like and it would be far more likely to enlighten the mind and touch the heart than your highest and best theological treatment of the doctrine of the Atonement.

Our Lord spoke in parables, just that men might not think they understood by learning dogmatic phrases or accepting truths too abstract to touch their lives. Where, for example, is there a theological exposition of all that is meant by pardon like the father waiting and running to meet his erring son and embracing him and overwhelming him with tokens of regard, with only the one all-sufficient requirement that he had returned home?

Though this does not mean that you are to shun large evangelical central texts, it does mean that, even with them, you are to try to embody the mood, the relation to life, the inmost spirit, and not merely the bare, disembodied spectre of the doctrine.

We have already considered the danger of falling into monotony of mood. If you concern yourself not only with the varied approach to life in your texts, but with their moods, and use them as key-notes, few things will do more to make you responsive to all the moods of the human soul and to all the range of experience by which God stirs to varied music its heart-strings. Especially, when possibly you fall into a mood too sad and despairing, and can hear in life only ' the still sad music of humanity,' the trumpet-note of triumph, which is never long wanting in Scripture, may be very grateful to your hearers, as well as an emancipation for your own spirit.

In the deepest sense texts must choose themselves, for they will never speak through you unless they have first spoken to you. Yet they do not always choose themselves well by the first impression, or by your immediate mood or present interest. Their value may be to succour you from monotony of mood and narrowness of interest. Wherefore what you most need may be as treasure hid in a field, which you can find only at the cost not of study alone but of selling your immediate interests to buy better. For this reason, if you begin a subject do not readily give it up, but persist in it till your mind and heart respond to it. Only by such resolute purpose are you ever likely to be able to declare the whole counsel of God. And even so, it is well to look over your past work to see whether you may not be neglecting central truths or failing to respond to God's manifold inspirations.

Even superficial reasons for choosing a text, such as that it is curious or misunderstood or two that are seemingly contradictory, may be defended. A text merely curious, if it arrest attention, be memorable and help to make truth near and living, may be profitable, if singularity of text is not made to do duty for sincerity of thinking.

Yet it is not a lasting device to resort to cleverness to escape the commonplace. Good preaching, like good poetry, does not deal with paradoxes and quirks and quiddities and pretty unexpected turns, but with the unrivalled glory and splendour of God's common world of men and things under God's common but infinitely changing sky of eternal truth.

Here then is the conclusion of the whole matter : the best text is that which has for you most inspiration, and especially for lifting the commonplace into the elemental. Though this may also provide most matter, the elemental is not the spacious. This last has its attractions because there are timid souls who suffer from claustrophobia and the one demand they make of a text is to ' give them room and verge enough.' Their ideal would be the ancient classical example, ' What is Man ? ' ' Man is a lost and ruined creature by the Fall,' and so on through the whole gamut of theology. Here also the strait gate leads to life and the broad road to destruction.

Your task as a teacher will nevertheless not have been fulfilled if you leave your hearers with the idea that the Bible is just a collection of edifying texts. If you could enable them so to read the Scriptures with understanding, with interest, with insight, that they may discover it to be of divine inspiration and profitable for teaching,

for reproof, for correction, for discipline in righteousness, and if thereby the man of God is made complete,
thoroughly furnished to every good work, even if this
should not be all your ministry, it would be its greatest
enrichment.

Perhaps, without some gift for this task and diligence
in using it, no minstry can have sufficient scope to
be of increasing interest and influence. Inspiration is
not a hebdomadal function, but if you yourself are
thoroughly furnished, you can be profitable for teaching
at all times.

The question of how you are to do it is of less
consequence than your knowledge of the subject and
interest in it, for if you are so equipped you will manage
it somehow.

Part of this at least is some reasonably adequate
knowledge of the light that the vast labour of scholars
has shed on it. The pulpit is not the place for discussing, let us say, the documents of the Pentateuch or
the sources of the Gospels, and none of it should be
done in such a way as to confirm the idea of some
good people that all criticism is merely 'tearing the
Bible to pieces.' But knowledge of it will save you
from many 'foolish and unlearned questions' and you
will be better able to show the relation of revelation
to life.

The same man who said he was weary to death of
hearing of love also said that he had been reading through
the Bible with some modern helps and was amazed to
find how astonishingly great and interesting a book
criticism had made it, as he had never learned from
all the ministries he had ever attended. And as it is
possible to make the Bible more vivid, more humanly
vital and more of a progressive revelation, not merely
historically but practically, by the aid of such knowledge, it should at least be attempted.

Lecturing is, of course, one method. As some lecture
when they profess to preach, and some preach when
they profess to lecture, the difference is between seeking

primarily to be edifying or to be instructive, not in length of text, but in aim and treatment.

You must have your own message, from your own experience to the experience of others, and to this even the Bible is subordinate. But your own experience will be the greater and your appeal to the experience of others wider and deeper, if enlarged by the whole experience of the saints.

When people knew their Bibles well, it was easy to interest them in it, and even pretty dull exposition could be followed with interest. But if the ignorance to-day is a difficulty, it only makes the duty of doing your best to enlighten it the more urgent.

The old method of exposition verse by verse can still be done by a few people with special gifts, though even in the old days it was apt to leave people in the position of a good old farmer after a long-drawn-out exposition of Colossians. "They Colossians," he said, "must have been very clever folk. If, as we were told, the epistle was just a letter written to be read to them, I suppose they would understand it when they heard, while we have been three months at it and don't understand it yet." To-day your success would be still more problematical.

Somehow none the less it ought to be possible to show that the Bible is a library of great religious literature, each book of it a message to its own age and having a message still for ours. To fail will be no proof of your ministry; and you will not fail if you have first-hand knowledge and the interest which first-hand knowledge alone can inspire.

But the Word of God is something which even the Bible only serves, and no writer of it ever made any claim except that he did so serve it. The prophets spoke the authentic Word of God, though they never appealed to any written authority, and never assumed any authority for their own writings except the appeal to the soul of the burden of the Lord. Though Jesus was so profound a student of the Old Testament that some have argued that He was addressed as Rabbi because He was one, He never appealed to its authority and He had a word for which its authority was of no avail : and all the more for this, both in His life and teaching the Word of God is manifest to all who will do it. St Paul no doubt, like Apollos, was mighty in the Scriptures, and he sometimes argued with the Jews on the ground of it. But this is far from being the most inspired Word of God he ever uttered. With the Gentiles, who were his special care, appeal to Scripture could have no weight : and it is just when he delivers to them what he calls his own gospel that the Word of the Lord, though to the Jews a stumbling-block and to the Greeks foolishness, had the demonstration of the Spirit by being the power of God unto salvation.

The Word of God concerns the rule of God amid which we live, known according as we live in it. As this includes all life and all things, our seeing of its whole scope is endless and seen only darkly, though its central truth is one and, in a sense, simple.

Both of the truth itself and knowledge of it there is no better account than that which closes the prophecies of Hosea. The sum of it is that, in spite of all the seeming success of violence and evil, of which Hosea had had ample experience both in his public and his private life, it is mercy and righteousness not violence and evil which rule the world, and that this is seen by wisdom and proved by practice.

Obviously this is either the greatest truth man ever discovered, or the greatest illusion he ever cherished, and there can be nothing between. Equally obviously it could be no inference from things as they are. Assyria gathered the nations as one gathers eggs, and riding on horses was irresistible might, as organised domination seems to be in our time. How then can anyone fail to say to the work of human hands ' Ye are our Gods,' or think that in God those utterly helpless in face of it find mercy. It was a victorious faith for Hosea precisely because it went against appearances, and it will not be otherwise in our time. In the deepest sense it cannot be taught ; but he who is wise—meaning the spiritually discerning—understands these things, and he who is prudent—meaning the skilled in applying them—knows them to be true. They are the things of righteousness and peace and joy in the Holy Spirit: and you will know them to be the ways of God in which, if a man walk, he stands and, if he leave, he falls, by discerning them and walking in them. Faith goes against appearances, not by betaking itself to other appearances like external authorities, but, as the prophets learned it, by digging down to the true meaning of life and listening to the voice of God in all their conduct of it. This was how the Bible was inspired and why it was a long process of enlightening prophetic souls, and not a word dictated at once from heaven as Mohammed professed to have received the Koran.

It was a long discovery of the fuller meaning of mercy not might ruling the world. By hearing eternal truth above all the tumult of the world prophetic souls knew and still know. Though eternity alone will be the final proof. Time also has not wholly failed to justify Hosea's conviction. Assyria, perhaps the most brutal exhibition of violence the world ever saw, has vanished without leaving behind a wrack of anything to enrich mankind, while Hosea's work is still a consolation and inspiration, still applicable to life and still proved true by right living. The worship of the work of men's own hands in our time will have a like ending, because though the ways of the Lord are long ways seeing He will not overcome might with might, they are right ways, and right ways alone are sure ways. This was the faith according to which the prophets had no other gods before God. Christ is the fulness of God's Word, because He is the perfect commendation of God's mercy and the victory over all evil which, in face of all that can be against us, makes the joy of the Lord our strength. He is the Word of God not only because He manifests God's rule, but also because He manifests it in God's way, by commending His love in face of all that seems to deny it.

Thus the Word of God was known and proved in the

past, and it is not otherwise in the present : and as it is known and proved, so is it to be taught and applied.

The Word of God is the mind of God, and therefore requires us to fulfil His will. Yet it is not as a commandment contained in ordinances, but by good news of One Whose will is for our good always.

The task of preaching is not merely to commend what is pious but to manifest what is true, which you do as it becomes good news, in one inseparable appeal to conscience of truth and conscience of right : and only when the truth so appeals that by it man may live triumphantly is it manifested as good news.

The other day I read this aphorism, " The secret of the best success is to make a fine art of doing well what you don't like." Though we might all with profit learn it better, because the merely pleasurable and the right are seldom in accord, we never do anything really well except we have joy in doing it, and no duty is rightly discharged merely as disagreeable drudgery.

Duty has been associated with distressful effort, not merely from making it the ground of merit, merit being in proportion to burden, but partly also by what I have called a neuralgic conscience, which identifies the distressing with the obligatory. Though this is better than identifying the obligatory with one's own likings, and you must deal gently with it, it is not life's sure guide, which is both wise and gracious.

There is a verse in the Psalms which says, " Thy statutes have been my songs in the house of my pilgrimage." Not God's promises, but His requirements are to be cheerful and cheering songs, not sombre dirges.

To many this union of song and duty seems mere incongruity. If conscience did not make cowards of us, with its hedging in of our way with thorns, how joyously should we wander along life's pleasant by-paths ! Is it not maintained that art is one thing and morality another, and even that they are opposites, one for pleasure, the other possibly for profit, but for painful profit ?

But about what have the really great poets sung?
Though as sensitive souls they have sometimes fallen
before temptation, have they ever lacked deep spiritual
and moral insight, or ever doubted the overwhelming
significance of the moral order or appealed to anything
save man's highest aspirations? They have often sung
of patient endurance in maintaining against overwhelming odds the right cause, and sometimes even of defeat
in the conflict. The glorious triumph of the oppressor,
the security of his power to inflict wrong, the ruth-
lessness which accumulates millions, in spite of their
many admirers, have yet to find a bard to celebrate
their successes. The poets have sung of human love,
but they have also made it the symbol whereby to
interpret all things. If only might is right, what would
be left for song in life's grim battle? The only music
would be the shout of them that triumph and the shriek
of them that perish. In the short dark night of our
pilgrimage, there is really nothing else to lift our hearts
to song save God's statutes, meaning by them His whole
government of the world, not His mere rules, so that no
life in it is truly blessed except by the guidance of truth
and righteousness.

It has been said, " Let me make the people's songs,
and anyone else can make their laws that likes." If
you could turn God's statutes into song, there would
be no need for laws. Not only are they the greatest
songs that have ever been sung, but unless they are
singing in men's hearts, other statutes will only be a
slavery to be flung off at the first opportunity. If your
preaching serves even a little to this end of making duty
a song, it will be a truly high calling on which you have
entered.

Preaching and worship, therefore, should not be set
over against one another, as if one had to do wholly
with man for his edification and the other wholly with
God for His adoration. God is glorified in the edification of His children and His children are edified as they
glorify God. You only praise aright when you know the

God Whom you adore and you only pray aright when you know the mind of Him to whom you pray ; and you only preach aright when you lift up men's souls to praise and stir in them the great spiritual needs which drive them to prayer. And even the sacraments are not rites separate and apart but are ' visible words,' deriving meaning and efficacy from the truth and worship and consecration they express and enforce to the mind and heart of the participant, the crown of all as they embody all.

It is your business to be as popular as you can and appeal to as wide an audience as you can, granting always that it is not at the price of lowering and cheapening your message. When a congregation becomes a select coterie of a special type of devout people, it may be leaven, but it is not in the meal. No congregation is for itself, but to be a light to all that are in the house, and if you have hearers who remain in the dim penumbra, it is your business to give them what light you can, and rejoice in their presence.

The question is, What is lowering and cheapening your message ? Is it anything less than coming short of declaring the whole counsel of God, anything less than persuading men of the truth of His whole mind in Jesus Christ and His whole purpose with men, and calling them to the service of His kingdom ? It should be a ministry of consolation, but it should not stop there, or even at the highest personal edification. And when it is mere temporary impression, collecting a crowd by fleeting interest and doing nothing to create a fellowship in the good news, which feels called to serve the glory of God in the good of His children, it does less.

With the latter conception of the ministry you would probably find it necessary to be continually on the move, with the former you probably would not. Yet there are few tasks in which it is more necessary to measure time ' by heart-beats, not by figures on a dial.' The Apostle's longest ministry in one place was three years, but as during that time he ceased not to warn everyone

Q

day and night with tears, few who attain their jubilee could rival it. Our Lord's whole ministry was perhaps only half that time, yet it was filled with all the fulness of God. The more ordinary the man, however, the more time he may need, though the more difficult he will find it to continue. But tasks are usually difficult in proportion as they are important. Still it is less a question of years than of a message the years cannot exhaust, not only because it concerns the eternal, but also because it embraces the whole significance of the temporal.

Unfortunately for the influence of congregations the members are nearly as migratory as their ministers, and the economic distribution in large cities hinders them from being the valuable link between rich and poor that they used to be. But difficulties only exist to be overcome, and it is your business to do all you can to overcome them. Wisdom is understanding to see the opportunity before you, and it is a fool's eyes that are in the ends of the earth.

> Type of the wise who soar but never roam
> True to the kindred points of heaven and home.

And if you would be at home among the people among whom God has placed you, you must remember in all your intercourse with them that a merry heart doeth good like a medicine, but a broken spirit drieth the bones.

In the end you must measure success not by

> The fame which in broad rumour lies,

but by that which

> Lives and spreads aloft by those pure eyes
> And perfect witness of all judging Jove.

Or, as the Apostle puts it more simply, in the sight of God and having your praise of Him and not of men.

That is a searching test, for God Who looks on the heart may know how poor are the springs of what outwardly may seem high devotion. Yet, as the Apostle did, you should think of it rather for your encouragement and peace, not only because it should deliver you from all petty vanities, from all efforts after cheap popularity, from any temptation to trim your message and lower it to make it more acceptable, but still more in that you can be assured that God knows, if man does not, that you have aimed high even when you have shot low, that you have laboured patiently even when there has been poor result, that if you have failed it has been through no slackness, and that if you have not managed to travel all the way, it has neither been through fear nor faintness of heart. And sometimes you may even cherish the hope that you have succeeded best in the thing whereto He really sent you, when in human eyes you seem only to have most suffered defeat.

INDEX

Printed by Turnbull & Spears, Edinburgh